Special Moments

Special Moments

GLORIA KEARNEY

Special Moments
© Copyright 2000 Gloria Kearney
By the same author "Sing in the Shadow" 1999

The Cobbles,
17 Lecale Park
Downpatrick BT30 6ST

All rights reserved

ISBN 1 84030 095 7

Ambassador Publications
a division of
Ambassador Productions Ltd.
Providence House
Ardenlee Street,
Belfast,
BT6 8QJ
Northern Ireland
www.ambassador-productions.com

Emerald House
427 Wade Hampton Blvd.
Greenville
SC 29609, USA
www.emeraldhouse.com

*This book is dedicated to
my new granddaughter, Ellie Niamh.
May she also one day walk with the Master.*

~ • ~

My thanks to:

*my long-suffering family, who cheerfully put up with all sorts of
hardship so that I could write*

*my prayer partners and other friends who encouraged me to have
this book published*

my son, Lysander, who drew the illustrations

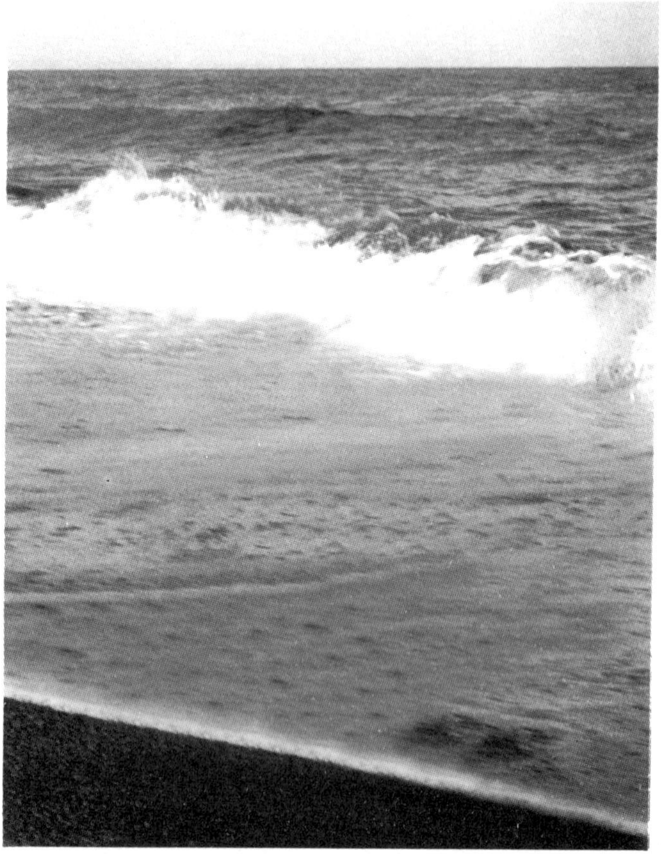

Special Moments

Clear skies, balmy evenings, the blue-green of the Mediterranean - Spain was everything it had promised to be and more! It was a memory-making fortnight - long, lazy days unwinding after a busy year at school, quiet times in the early morning, on a sunlounger beside a palm tree lined pool, the excitement of visiting the ancient Palace of Alhambra, the Rock of Gibraltar, the filmset in the middle of the Tavernes Desert. All of these I enjoyed to the full but for me there were one or two special moments, fleeting little unexpected bonuses that I felt in my spirit were gifts from a Father who specialises in delighting His children.

The first of these took place late at night. We had spent most of the day travelling along the south coast of Spain, stopping for short visits to the caves of Nerja and the mountain village of Mijas. We had enjoyed to the full a boat trip from the harbour at Marbella and the lavish evening meal at the hotel booked for our overnight stay. Darkness had fallen by the time we finished but we decided to take a walk along the beach. I was pleased to discover that the sand was soft and fine, not like the shingle of the beach in the resort where we were staying. So my sandals were hurriedly discarded as I made my way down to the sea.

I knew as I paddled in the warm water along the edge of the sea that I would remember that scene for a long time. The beach was almost deserted, the sunloungers were stacked under the grass matting umbrellas, there was little sound except for the gentle swish of the tiny waves as they broke on the shore, the air was warm and an almost full moon shone from a black velvet sky. It was a moment of breathtaking beauty, a special moment.

Yet another occurred on the way back to Almeria on that same trip. The coach pulled in to the car park beside the caves of Nerja for a short break in the five hour journey. The guide reminded us about the garden beside the entrance to the caves and I decided to sit for a while in the shade of the trees. In the middle of the garden a large curved stone bench had been built into the bank and my son and I made our way there to rest in the shade.

I hadn't noticed until we got closer to the bench that two men were already sitting there. They were tuning guitars and as we sat on the cool stone, they began to play. One picked out a lovely haunting Spanish melody while his friend provided exciting backing rhythms to accompany it. The heat of the day and the discomfort of the long journey were forgotten as I looked around at the green ferns and palm trees that had been planted nearby and allowed the beauty of the music to wash over me. Beautiful music and exquisite surroundings are a heady mixture - they made a very special moment.

My life with Jesus has been a little similar to my Spanish holiday. I have enjoyed to the full much of the thirty-nine years I have walked with Him. I have wonderful memories of exciting places we have visited together and I can also recall times when the heat and discomfort of the journey were hard to bear, but now and again there have been moments that have stood out for me - moments when I have sensed the Father reaching out to me from the edge of eternity to delight my heart with a special moment. Most of the chapters in this book were written as a result of the special moments God has given me.

As we walk together through the many rooms in my Father's House, I pray that you too will experience moments that will be special to you, little love gifts from above.

SECTION ONE
In My Father's House

The Gate

The Banqueting Hall

The Robe Chamber

The Music Room

The Throne Room

The Perfumery

The Kitchen

The Building Site

The Armoury

The Storehouse

Picnic in the Valley

The Rose

The Library

The Waiting Room

*... only one entrance, a narrow gate
at the foot of a cross ...*

The Gate

The magnificence and beauty of the Father's House can never be fully appreciated while we remain on this side of eternity. The creation of this amazing universe in which we live took only six days but Jesus told His disciples that He was going to prepare a place for us in His Father's House and that work has been going on for almost two thousand years! There is just no concept of magnificence wonderful enough to even begin to describe the Father's House.

Occasionally, at some special moment or in some particular circumstance, the Father grants us a glimpse of His House in this life, a tiny peep around the edge of a door that lies slightly ajar. Even that fleeting glimpse is almost too much for us. We find ourselves overawed by the majestic splendour we perceive and overwhelmed by the encompassing love we encounter.

We first enter His House through the Gate of Salvation. There may be many rooms in this wonderful house but there is only one entrance, a narrow gate at the foot of a cross.

Join me in a moment which, though rooted in reality, an actual moment in history, is also in a strange way a timeless moment. In the past two thousand years many feet have walked the path we are about to follow and many people have acknowledged their arrival at the Cross to be not just a special moment, but also a defining moment in their lives, a pivotal moment after which everything changed - direction and focus and purpose. Come, let's make our way up Calvary's Hill.

It is a bit of a climb and you feel a little confused as you walk along. Part of you doesn't really want to climb the hill and face what you know to be at the top but something draws you irresistibly along. You push your way through the groups of people crowding around - men shouting abuse, jeering; soldiers standing impassive, bored with yet another crucifixion; another little group crying bitterly, wailing at the loss of a friend.

Suddenly, there it is before you - a rough wooden cross. As your fearful gaze travels to the top you can see Him hanging there - Jesus - alone, weak, vulnerable, broken, dying in agony. The ugliness of what you see hurts you.

Jesus, the Son of God, on a cross. It seems all wrong somehow and you want to cry out,

"Take Him down! How could this have happened?"

The One by whom all things were made, in whom all things hold together - the Glorious Son of the Living God - on a cross? Why did it have to be like this?

The answer brings no comfort - it was your sin. Your sin that caused His shame, His suffering, His separation from the Father. You turn away, your sense of guilt so strong that you are desperate to escape, to leave this awful place, but as you turn, you catch a glimpse of His face. You look again and there you see only love and acceptance from the One who died in your place, and with tears running down your face, you kneel in repentance and worship at His feet.

In that instant, you find yourself on the other side of the Gate and there before you, stretching as far as the eye can see, is the magnificence of the Father's House. You sense somehow, without ever being told, that the rest of your life will be an amazing adventure spent in the company of the One whose love has so recently overwhelmed your spirit.

It is thirty-nine years since I stood at the narrow gate and knelt before the cross of Jesus but I can still recall the tremendous joy of knowing the extent of His love for me. I determined that day to follow the Master. From time to time since then, the Master has taken me by the hand and led me on a tour of the corridors in His House and the grounds of His Estate. I know that what I see behind the doors is only a tiny glimpse and I am aware that I could never hope to reflect even a small part of the full glory of these rooms, but the glimpses have been a source of rich blessing and encouragement.

My heartfelt thanks to the Master.

Before Your Cross

I stand before Your cross in awe,
Amazed at what I see,
This day of anguished sorrow
Imparts rich happiness to me.

Forgiveness flows so freely,
From the One blamed in the wrong,
He is cast aside, rejected,
I stand accepted fully, I belong.

He covers me in mercy,
And clothes me with His grace,
While He is stripped of all He owned,
He hangs there, nearly naked, in disgrace.

Adopted, now a joint-heir with His Son,
The Father welcomes me with all His heart,
While Jesus suffers separation,
The loneliness of God, from God apart.

He freely gives His spirit unto death,
I cannot understand the reason why,
The only way I'm giv'n eternal life,
Is for the King of Glory so to die.

So much He gives, so much I gain,
Such joy for me, for Him such pain,
I stand in awe to see such grace,
Open my heart, His love to embrace.

The Banqueting Hall

I was not long settled in my new home when a messenger brought an invitation to me - a special, gilt-edged invitation, bearing the King's seal. I opened it eagerly and was delighted to discover that the King Himself had invited me to a banquet in His Banqueting Hall.

My joy and excitement were soon subdued as I realised that I had no suitable clothes for such a grand occasion and I began to think,

"I won't be able to go to the banquet."

My heart was sad but then I remembered some words from the Rule Book of the Kingdom - a promise that the King Himself would clothe His people with garments of salvation.

Some time later I set off for His Banqueting Hall, now suitably dressed and full of excitement at the thought of the promised banquet. My heart sang as I walked along.

As I walked towards the hall, I began to wonder what it would be like at the banquet - who else had been invited? What would the Banqueting Hall be like? Would I see the King? Would I perhaps even get a chance to speak to Him?

I arrived at the magnificently carved, double doors, my name was announced, the doors were flung open and there before me was the banqueting table, laden with all the riches of the kingdom - bowls filled with love, plates heaped high with grace, cups of salvation, fellowship and mercy - what an amazing feast!

As I lifted my gaze from the banqueting table itself, I began to realize that no one else was there. Was I the first to arrive? Surely the King would have invited hundreds to share in this feast?

Then I heard His voice calling from the other end of the long banqueting table,

"Come," He said, "sit by My side."

As I moved at His bidding, I began to understand that this was not to be a banquet for hundreds - He had set up His banqueting table just for me; He had provided these amazing riches just for me. At this table there would only be myself and my King, the Master.

I knelt before Him in worship.

Knowing Him

God calls us to know Him.
We know Him in the stillness.

In the stillness of a friendship
where words are not needed,
In the security of a relationship
where being together is enough,
In the beauty of a closeness
where love has no need to be expressed.

The special moment at which I caught a glimpse into the Robe Chamber happened during a prayer time with my prayer partners, Lavinia and Pat. In her prayer, Lavinia quoted the verse from Isaiah ch 61 which says,
"For He has clothed me with garments of Salvation and arrayed me in a Robe of Righteousness."
Pat then followed that quotation with another from Colossians ch 3,
"Therefore......... clothe yourselves with compassion, kindness, humility, gentleness and patience."
As they prayed I could just see the wonderful image of the Master placing His magnificent Robe of Righteousness on my shoulders and I was given fresh insight into the lavish grace He bestows freely on His children.

The Robe Chamber

The Master called me to the Robe Chamber, and there I stood before Him in my old, filthy rags, feeling vulnerable and ashamed.

He took from the riches of His storehouse, a robe and held it out to me.

"Wear my robe of righteousness," He said.

It was a gown of great magnificence, woven from the finest thread of loving sacrifice, designed and made by the Master Craftsman, the Creator of heaven and earth.

As it slipped over my head and settled on my shoulders I could see that it fitted perfectly and covered me completely. Overcome by the magnitude of such a gift, I twirled and leaped for joy and felt the tender caress of the fabric as I moved. How good it felt to be wearing His righteousness.

He threw away my ill-fitting, ragged shoes and from His bounteous store of grace, He took out and placed on my tired and aching feet, soft shoes of peace.

"Now", He said, "wherever I will send you, you will walk in peace."

I was still taking my first few tentative steps, trying out my shoes of peace, when the Master spoke again.

"I have a cloak for you - wear it often, use it well."

He threw around my shoulders an unbelievably beautiful garment - a garment of praise. Long and flowing, fashioned from a thousand silvery tones, it shimmered and shone and caused my heart to sing in worship and adoration. I drew its soft folds about me and vowed to wear it all the time.

Then, light as gossamer, I sensed Him place - was it a veil? - over my head. It was so pure and fine that it was almost invisible yet I could sense the reality of this wondrous veil by the rainbow reflections of His light upon it.

"I have clothed you in My glory," were the words He said.

Amazed and awed by what He had done for me, I turned to go, but the Master's voice called me back.

"The robes I have given you are free - the cost was met by My Son. Wear them with joy in your heart. They will never fade, wear thin, or be taken from you."

"But there is something you must do. You will be aware of My robe of righteousness, My shoes of peace, My cloak of praise, My veil of glory but they will remain invisible to others. So I'm sending you some other garments. My desire is that you should choose to put them on each day. Unlike My other gifts, they may wear thin or fade or need to be renewed. Come often to My storehouse for fresh supplies".

"How will I know what to ask for?" I whispered.

"Their names are compassion, kindness, humility, gentleness, patience and love. When you wear these, others will see a reflection of My glory."

"So go, clothed in My righteousness, walking in peace, wearing praise as a garment and sharing My glory".

"...that we may know Him who is true......"

I would know my God,
Amazed though I may be
That He should have the least desire
To know one such as me.

I would know my God,
I long to hear His voice,
To sense deep in my spirit
Truths that make my heart rejoice.

I would know my God,
Know the wonder of His love,
Know Him as my greatest Friend,
Who pours out riches from above.

I would know my God,
Oh how I long to know Him more,
To feel the sweetness of His touch,
Know all the bounties in His store.

I would know my God,
Whose glory I can share,
Who covers me with mercy,
Gives me righteousness to wear.

I shall know my God,
One day I'll gaze into His face,
Then for everlasting years,
I'll know the fulness of His grace.

The scene of this special moment was a midweek prayer meeting. We were singing the chorus "Lord make me an instrument, an instrument of worship" and suddenly I could see us all - an orchestra of living instruments, some more tuneful than others, some more obedient to the Conductor's baton than others, but all committed to bringing glory to the Father by the music we made together.

*... together we played an eternal symphony
the song of the ages ...*

The Music Room

As we walked through the endless corridors of His house, I began to hear in the distance, faint snatches of a melody, played with such grace and charm that my heart ached to be one with those who produced the interweaving harmonies. My longing must have been communicated to the One who walked with me, for He stopped outside a room and motioned me inside,

"Come in." He said, "this is My Music Room."

I stepped eagerly inside and was instantly filled with intense delight as the wonderful music flowed around me. I looked quickly from one side of the room to the other to find the instruments that were being played so skilfully but saw only people - men and women, boys and girls. I turned to question the Master and He smiled at my bewilderment.

"My orchestra is like no other. The players have no instruments - instead the players are the instruments. Let Me introduce you to a few of them."

"That first group on the left at the front - they are My first violins - the leaders of My orchestra. Theirs is an awesome responsibility - to work hard, to learn the music well, to constantly watch the Conductor's signals and interpret them correctly. Their position requires great sensitivity to the music and confident leadership. Because of where they sit, if they make a mistake, it is immediately obvious to everyone in the auditorium. But when the symphony is over, it is to them that I first reach out My hand to acknowledge the part they have played."

I glanced at their faces, alight with devotion and commitment - they obviously knew the Conductor and trusted Him completely.

Then He drew me over to the woodwind section and pointed out a group of ladies who were chattering animatedly. With amusement in His voice, He said,

"Meet My piccolos. They may be small, seem insignificant and their tone may be a little shrill at times but they are the highest, brightest instruments and when the moment comes for them to play the melody, their voices can be heard above the whole orchestra."

Some portly gentlemen stood quietly nearby, in sharp contrast to the excited piccolos. Their lives sang out a low, rich sound.

"My double basses and My tubas," He explained. "They rarely play a solo part but instead are content to provide the bass line - a solid foundation on which My symphony can be based."

With a grand, sweeping gesture, He then indicated those who stood along the back - a very busy group, most of them young, all making a tremendous sound. I had the distinct impression that He revelled in their noise and excitement.

"Meet the percussion instruments - bass drums, snare drums, cymbals, gong, tambourines, bells, maracas. They're loud and noisy, sometimes hard to listen to. Some are very limited, only producing a single sound and that not even a musical sound. Many of these instruments cannot play a tune, only beat a rhythm. But if they beat to My rhythm, what colour and excitement is added to the music."

By this time I was so filled with delight that I could scarcely contain it and wanted simply to know how and when I could join in and wondered which instrument I would become. The Master anticipated my question.

"Don't be too concerned with how I shall use you. Every instrument was bought by My Son and I love each one with equal passion and devotion. You may begin as one instrument and by the end of the symphony be another one entirely. Just be content that I will use you."

I listened once again to the music of this amazing symphony, music that sang out the story of redemption, music composed before the dawn of time. I heard the mellow clarinets, the soothing tones of the flutes, the richness of the cellos, the strident voices of the trumpets, the melancholic violins, the cheerful, tinkling sounds of the glockenspiels, the clashing cymbals, the dancing rhythms of the maracas and wondered that this diversity of instruments could blend into such unity of sound. I was afraid that when I sounded out my note, it would in some way spoil the harmony or interrupt the movement of the rhythm.

"Don't be afraid," He said, "All you need to do is follow the guidelines I'm going to give you. The beauty of My symphony depends on them."

"First there has to be submission to the music chosen for the orchestra to play, then, obedience to the Conductor's signals. Daily practice is essential, constantly striving to be better, to produce a purer tone, to learn new techniques. Stay tuned - every instrument tunes to the same note and great care is taken throughout the whole symphony to stay in tune."

"Be sensitive to your fellow musicians and to the music. Learn that there are times for strength and power and other times for gentleness and a delicate touch; there are times when you sing out the melody and times when you hold back to allow other players to tell the story. Listen to each other and learn to love their music as well as your own."

"Above all, persevere. Some sections of the symphony are difficult but don't stop playing. Instead, watch the Conductor with even greater diligence and allow His hand to guide you through the passages where the harmonies are complex and the melody is hard to play."

"Now come," He said, "Sing out your song for Me."

I fixed my eyes on His and softly played the part that He had written just for me. In that moment I knew my heart's desire fulfilled - my rhythm matched His beat, my harmony fitted His song, I was at one with the music all around me. Together we played an eternal symphony, the song of the ages, telling in a thousand different tunes the story of the Cross, of peace with God and of the joy of His Spirit. And as I moved to the beat of His heart, I knew His peace, felt His love and was filled with great joy at the realisation that I would sing His song for ever.

His Song, My Song

He gave to me a song,
And all the notes were given,
And all the harmonies I'd need
To sing my song from Heaven.

He said, "Come, sing your song,
When joy and peace are all you see.
But also sing when life is rough-
It still sounds sweet in a minor key."

I raised my voice and sang His song
And knew within, He sang with me,
My heart rejoiced to understand
I'd sing this song for eternity.

The Throne Room

"Master," I asked one day as we walked along together, "can You show me the Throne Room? I've heard so many other people in the Father's House talk about being to the Throne of Grace. Some seem to go there every day. Can You show me where to go?"

"You have only to ask, child," was the Master's reply. "Come with me."

We walked for a while then turned a corner into an area that was new to me. I caught a glimpse of the door and stopped in amazement. I had never seen a door quite like this one. It appeared to be made of solid gold yet the material was so delicate that the light from the room beyond shone through. The golden door shimmered as though moved by a gentle breeze and the movement caused the light to be reflected in a thousand different directions.

"Master," I whispered, "I don't think I'll go in."

"Why ever not?" He asked.

"The door in..... it scares me a little. It's just too wonderful. What must the room be like? I don't think I'm ready for such magnificence."

"Don't be afraid," was His reply, "I'll come with you."

So, rather tentatively, I approached the door and reached out my hand to open it, only to discover that this door had no handle.

"How do I get in?" I asked.

"Just say My name and walk right through."

Although I thought that it was a strange thing to do, I had learnt the value of obeying the Master so I quickly said His name and slowly began to walk towards the door. To my astonishment I was able to walk right through the golden door.

Once inside I immediately felt compelled to fall to my knees. The intensity of the light hurt my eyes and I was overcome by such a sense of my sin and my unworthiness that bowing down seemed somehow the only appropriate thing to do. In this room, more than in any other room, I sensed the holiness and majesty of the Father. The purity of His presence only increased my sense of shame yet at the same time I felt a warm enveloping welcome. I felt secure, I felt accepted, I felt loved.

Emboldened by this and consumed by curiosity, I raised my head to look around the Throne Room but immediately I did so, the Master moved to stand in front of me. Though I didn't like to complain, I gathered enough courage to whisper,

"Master, You're in my way, I can't see."

"I know, child," He said, "but there's a reason why I'm standing here. The Father cannot look at you because of the sin that has caused you so much shame. His justice would demand that your sin be punished by death. Neither can you look at Him for such is His holiness that you would not be able to bear to see it. So child, I will stand between you. When you look at Me, you can see the Father because the Father and I are one and when the Father looks at you, He sees Me, His own beloved Son, because your life is hidden in Mine. So don't be afraid, approach the Throne boldly, I'm covering you."

His words took away my fear and gave me such confidence that I moved on further into the room and knelt before the Throne of Grace. I wasn't sure what to do next and looked enquiringly at the Master.

"Just say what is in your heart," He suggested.

So I told the Father what was in my heart - my sense of awe and wonder at finding myself before His Throne, my gratitude for the welcome I experienced, the debt of love I owed to the Master for making it all possible. The more I talked to the Father, the more at ease I felt and soon I found myself confessing to Him my weaknesses and my failures. As I did so, forgiveness instantly flowed from the Throne, washing over me again and again, bringing cleansing and healing and a renewed determination to find my strength in the One who had bought my forgiveness with His blood. Suddenly I became aware of a strange heaviness upon my heart and I started to panic.

"What is it, Master? What has gone wrong? Why do I feel this way? I think my heart is going to break."

"You're feeling a burden, child. Nothing is wrong. It happens sometimes when you stay close to the Throne of Grace. The Father has entrusted a burden to you. You must pray fervently for what He puts on your heart. It's how He changes things in your world. Be faithful and watch carefully and you'll see Him at work."

So I prayed for the burden He had put on my heart, for people and situations as His Spirit brought them to my mind - for the healing of a friend, for the protection of a loved one, for peace in my homeland. The more I prayed, the less I felt the weight of the burden.

"The Father will give you different burdens for different times," the Master continued. "Learn to recognise the heaviness as a prompting to pray."

As the burden lessened, it seemed as though words left me and I knelt for a long time in silence. A great calm descended on my spirit and I had no desire to break the peace I was experiencing but after some time I became agitated in case my silence would displease the Father, that it would be disrespectful to stay silent at the Throne. The Master sensed my disquiet and reassured me,

"Your silence is as much an offering of worship as your words. It's only in the silence He can speak to you. Listen well to what He says in your heart."

So I listened and to my great delight, I heard His voice. It was, on this first time, the merest whisper, a faint stirring of compassion, the memory of a verse from His Word but I knew it was His voice. And I knew that as I came more often to His Throne, I would hear His voice more clearly. I rose and made my way back through the golden door, rejoicing in the knowledge that I carried His voice, His Word in my heart. How privileged I was to live in His House and have such access to His Throne of Grace.

Anna

Anna knew how to stay in His presence,
In the Temple day after day,
Her life was a life full of worship,
She knew how to fast and to pray.

Anna's feet never walked through the veil,
She never saw the lamb being slain.
Far back in the court of the women
She waited again and again.

And God came from the Holy of Holies
Walked on through the Holy Place,
Passed the men as they stood in the Temple,
Chose to meet Anna face to face.

And she knew the sound of His voice,
Heard it clearly despite all the din,
Had the courage to speak out the words
That the Spirit prompted within.

Oh meet with me as with Anna,
Speak to me, oh my Lord, face to face,
Bring me day after day to Your Presence,
Whisper words full of truth and of grace.

A sermon was the catalyst for this special moment - a sermon preached by my Pastor and friend, Hadden Wilson.

One Sunday morning he made a reference to the instructions given by God in Exodus ch 30 for the preparation of the priests' anointing oil. As I listened to the words the whole idea of the anointing oil caught my imagination. This was a unique oil, made from exotic ingredients, the formula for which was not to be used for any other perfume (on pain of death) and whose sole purpose was to anoint a priest.

The realisation that the oil with which He anoints His children, His own Holy Spirit, is even more precious, led to the concept of the Perfumery.

The poem that follows tells a true story.

A few years ago Rachel Hickson was one of the seminar speakers at Focusfest, a women's conference that takes place in Northern Ireland each year. She is a passionate speaker and as she prayed at the end of her seminar, I could feel the tears rising up within me. I don't cry easily so it was all the more unusual to find myself sobbing, unable to stop. I knew that I was crying for the people of our church and for our much-loved Pastor but I sensed that the tears were more than just my emotional response to passionate preaching - they were, I felt, an expression of God's heart. Other ladies from the church were there and we all gathered round to pray and cry together.

It was a most unusual experience which, so far, has not been repeated but I believe that it gave me a little insight into the heart of God and His longing that His people would know the anointing of His Spirit upon them.

32

... but why is Love in such a tiny bottle? ...

The Perfumery

We left the Music Room, stepping out once more into the endless corridors of the Master's house. We turned a corner and slowly I became aware that the air all around was filled with the most wondrous aroma. The Master, whom I now realized had immediate access to my every thought, looked at me and said,

"Yes, it's beautiful. Come, I want to show you My Perfumery."

The sweet smell permeating the air grew stronger as He opened a door until it seemed I would be overcome completely by the mingling of scents assailing my senses. The Master motioned to a chair,

"Sit quietly," He said, "allow the fragrance to enrich your inner being. It is the fragrance of My own Beloved Son."

The room was small, and every wall was lined from floor to ceiling with shelves on which stood jars and bottles of every conceivable size and shape and colour. Although each one was firmly stoppered, the sweet scents could not be contained inside but filtered slowly through the corks into the room.

I gazed along the shelves and in among the scents I recognized from earth, the rose, honeysuckle, cinnamon and frankincense, I read the names of other fragrances.

"What's this?" I wondered, "Loyalty, righteousness, compassion? These are perfumes?"

"Perfumes of the sweetest kind," He said. He reached out to a bottle with the name "Integrity" etched into the glass. Removing the cork, He invited me to smell. It was like no fragrance ever known on earth - no flower or tree had ever smelt so sweet.

I looked more closely all along the shelves and soon my eye picked out humility and patience, kindness, tenderness and trust.

"But why is love in such a tiny bottle?" I enquired.

The Master smiled, "It is because it only takes a little drop of love to create a beautiful fragrance. It lasts for life, you see, and grows and multiplies within the heart."

As I continued to search, I came across a bottle of such unusual shape that I took it in my hand to examine it more closely.

"This looks like a horn," I said, "What is this perfume's name?"

"Ah you've found My horn of anointing oil," the Master answered. "In days of old I gave instructions for the manufacture of a special oil. Its formula was unique, it contained ingredients used in no other perfume. It had only one purpose - the anointing of My priests. So is the oil you are holding - unique, made from a special blend known only to the Father, having a sole purpose - the anointing of My people."

I knelt then in that tiny room and from my heart I cried, "I am Your child - pour out on my head Your oil of anointing."

He raised the horn and in a moment oil poured forth and mingled with my tears. Its fragrance was the sweet perfume of heaven, enriching and refreshing to my soul. Its touch began as a tender caress but it grew in intensity until it was a fire that burned into my soul, a cleansing, healing, strengthening fire.

"Now go, with My fire in your spirit, knowing the joy of My anointing in your soul. Enjoy the warmth of My spirit enriching your inner being as you worship Me. Be assured of the might of My spirit, empowering you as you work for Me."

I stepped somewhat reluctantly from that hallowed place and, as I walked away, the sweet aroma of His presence wafted all around. The oil of His spirit still flowed and little droplets fell at my feet, scenting my pathway.

I found that as I journeyed on, each time I reached out to another life, the oil was shared and passed along yet, like the widow's oil of old, it never was diminished and many lives were blessed. I also found, to my delight, that other souls had visited the Master's Perfumery. They were easily recognized for the fragrance of the room lingered around them and almost immediately, eyes met, hands clasped and a mutual love sprang up, agape reborn.

God Gave Me Tears

God gave me tears for you today,
He broke my heart in two,
The anguish that He gave to me,
Is how He feels for you.

His longing heart yearns after you,
I felt the pain He feels.
The sobs that tore into my soul,
His love for you reveals.

His horn of oil is ever poised
To spill out on your head.
"My Holy Spirit I will pour
Upon all flesh," He said.

You only have to whisper, "Come."
With joy His heart is filled,
For He delights to lavish grace,
To see His oil outspilled.

Oh stand and lift your face to Him
Oh let His oil flow free,
And know the Spirit's mighty power
Bring joy and liberty.

He would fill you with Himself.
What more could you desire?
Filled with the fulness of your God,
Touched by consuming fire.

Oh don't resist or turn away,
But grant Him full control,
May His Spirit light a fire,
To burn His brand upon your soul.

The poem that follows my glimpse into the Master's Kitchen was inspired by an exceptionally special moment about five years ago. At that time I was privileged to be part of a prayer triplet that had grown to a quartet and sometimes even a quintet and which proved to be a rich source of blessing to me. We met as usual that Friday night around Maisie's kitchen table, had a cup of tea, chatted for a while, shared some prayer requests and then began to pray. Part way through the evening, silence descended on our little group, not the sort of silence that indicates a barrier to prayer, but a silence imposed by the Father Himself as He makes His Presence an almost tangible reality. It lasted about three quarters of an hour and then we talked together about what God had said to us in the silence. We were awestruck to discover that God had whispered the same message to each of us as we sought to hear His voice. Moments like that are not easily forgotten.

The Kitchen

"Are you hungry?" the Master enquired as we entered yet another wing of this incredible mansion.

"Why, yes, I believe I am," I answered a little uncertainly. I had been experiencing strange pangs, and an unfamiliar emptiness since leaving the perfumery but couldn't be sure of their origin or their meaning. Perhaps the pangs were hunger pangs.

I followed as He pushed open a double swing door and stood for a moment, taking in the scene before me. I had entered a large, bustling kitchen, where small groups of busy people were positioned at various workstations, all engaged in preparing food, cooking food, or serving food. The room was warm and the air was filled with tantalizing smells - freshly baked bread, the rich herbs and spices flavouring casseroles and the tempting aroma of cakes cooling on wire racks.

As the pangs in my stomach increased in intensity and my mouth began to water, I realized that I had been hungry all along - I just hadn't recognized the feeling. I couldn't understand why this should be when I had known hunger many times before, so I looked to the Master for an explanation.

"What you are feeling now," He said so tenderly, "is not a natural hunger for natural food, but a spiritual hunger for spiritual food. You have a hunger in your soul for Me!"

He picked up one of the golden crusted loaves of bread and gently tore it apart.

"My Word," He said, "the bread that nourishes your relationship with Me. It's your staple food, fresh each day, providing nutrients for growth, strength and energy."

He broke off a piece and held it out to me. "Eat," He said. I took the bread and ate hungrily and it was sweet and soft in my mouth.

With a beckoning gesture, He invited one of the groups of busy cooks to bring their dish to the table at which we now sat. It looked like a rich, nutritious stew, a blend of good meat, fresh vegetables, pure water and exotic spices.

"The cooks in My kitchen are always kept busy preparing large quantities of this dish for My people. Its name is Truth."

One of the cooks served a generous portion of the dish into a bowl and pushed it towards me.

"I suggest a large portion of Truth at regular intervals - it will keep your soul in good health," He said, "though there are some who find it difficult to chew and hard to digest."

The dish was delicious. It had a strong flavour, a pungent smell and I felt immediate satisfaction as I chewed the meat and appreciated the rich sauce. I chewed carefully and thoughtfully and could understand why some might find this meal too heavy.

The Master then turned to another busy group and the head cook looked at Him pointedly before asking, "Are You sure, Master?"

"Yes, bring it over," was the reply.

Almost reluctantly, the cook served a tiny portion of this new dish and invited me to eat. I took a spoonful, then recoiled in shock - it had a bitter, unpleasant taste and was extremely hard to swallow.

The Master gave a wry smile, "No one enjoys this dish - its name is Rebuke. Sadly I have to serve it to My people quite often. I use it to sweeten temperament and build character."

I managed, albeit with some difficulty, to finish the portion allotted to me and wondered apprehensively what else was on the menu.

Suddenly three or four cooks came rushing over from various workstations. They placed on the kitchen table an amazing array of sweetmeats of all shapes and sizes. They were beautifully decorated in the colours of the rainbow. I could smell honey and mixed spice and cinnamon, strawberry and mango, lemon and lime.

My eyes sparkled and my mouth watered in anticipation as I looked for the Master's permission to eat.

"Go on," He said, "spoil yourself. These delicacies are called Encouragement. They are sweet to the taste, you will never tire of them. You can eat as many as you like and still want to come back for more."

He looked around the vast kitchen at all the people busy stirring pots or chopping food.

"I have more cooks preparing encouragement than anything else. These sweetmeats lift the spirits of those who are depressed or lonely, comfort the bereaved and the abused, give strength to the weary and the oppressed, calm the agitated and bring hope to the hopeless."

As He talked, He began to fill a candy box with some of the sweetmeats. These He passed across the table to me with the words, "Take these with you on the rest of the journey. Give them out freely to those whom you meet. You will bring light to their eyes, a smile to their lips and great delight to their souls."

At A Kitchen Table

The Lord Himself drew near,
Overwhelming in His awesome Might,
And each one knew His presence
As He met with us that night.

Stilled and quiet there before our God,
Awed into silence by His majesty,
Afraid to move, afraid almost to breathe,
Longing to hold that moment for eternity.

We found it hard to understand
That God, the Great Almighty God,
Should at a kitchen table choose to sit
And on our hearts should choose to write His word.

"Drink deeply" so His loving message came,
"My living water cleans and purifies.
Feed hungrily, come in your emptiness
You'll find that My word fills and satisfies."

And in His presence then we bowed,
Made solemn vows to God the Lord above.
"We will drink deep, feast richly on Your Word
And listen always for the whisper of Your love."

... why are You using such useless bricks? ...

The Building Site

I followed the line of the high wire fence until I came to a rough gate, constructed from scaffolding poles and fencing. I pushed it open and walked carefully on to the site. The place was a hive of activity; people scurrying to and fro, men in hard hats shouting instructions, lorry drivers delivering building materials, architects poring over drawings and plans. The Master was busy in the midst of it all so I went to watch what He was doing.

I found Him working at one corner of the structure and to my amazement, I realised that He was using living bricks. He gently placed a row of these living bricks on to the foundation, making sure that they were standing side by side, their shoulders touching. Almost as soon as He had turned His back, they began to elbow and jostle each other until each one stood independently, in his own space.

The Master frowned, but said nothing. He then positioned another row of living bricks on the shoulders of the first row, but in some places the space was too large and the brick fell through, landing with a dull thud on the ground below. I wasn't close enough to see but I felt sure that the brick must have been damaged. Eventually the first row realised what was happening, looked sheepishly at the Master and edged back into their original positions, standing closely together.

The Master continued to build, adding row after row of living bricks. The whole structure looked unstable, constantly shifting as the bricks tried to keep their balance. Suddenly one of the bricks on the top row scrambled down out of his place and ran to the other side. With a look of grim determination on his face, he pulled himself up towards a tiny space. I gasped in horror as I watched him push and shove his way into the space which was much too small for him. I cried out to warn the rest of the bricks on the top row but it was too late. He gave a final heave and pulled himself upright. The inevitable happened and the whole top row collapsed. I felt my stomach lurch as I heard the cries that went up from those who had fallen.

The Master walked across to where they lay and patiently proceeded to bind up their wounds with His special balm before replacing them along the top row. As I watched, I could see each living brick make a valiant effort to remain fixed in his place and none made a greater effort than the disobedient brick, now back in his original position.

For a little while the structure stood firm and I noticed some bystanders even began to go inside, seeking the shelter of its walls. Then suddenly, disaster struck. My eye caught a movement in the bottom row and I realised that someone's foot had slipped. He struggled to remain upright but it was no use and I watched helplessly as the whole structure collapsed in a great heap on top of those who had earlier sought refuge.

I couldn't bear to watch any more and called out to the Master in great distress. He came at once to my side and His presence calmed my agitation.

"Whatever are You building? Why are You using such useless bricks?" I asked.

"I'm building My church," He replied softly, "but as you can see, the materials I'm using are difficult to work with. They won't do as they are told, they won't stay where I have placed them and they so easily fall into sin. But they are Mine and I love them and I'll keep on building until it is complete."

"Of course," He went on, "it isn't always like this. Come and see."

And He led me to another corner of this incredible structure and invited me to watch while He built. This time the living bricks stood closely together in obedience to Him and each one remained where the Master put him. The strongest bricks were carefully placed in the bottom row and they braced themselves while the second row was placed on their shoulders. The structure still looked as though it would turn out to be just as unstable as the previous one I had seen but the Master encouraged me to continue watching.

"See, these living bricks have learnt a vital lesson."

As He placed the final brick in the second row I saw that each brick in the bottom row reached out both arms to encircle the shoulders of the bricks on each side and then grasped the feet of the bricks in the row above. The structure no longer swayed uncertainly for the bricks supported each other and so held firm. As the Master built, so the bricks intertwined and locked together until this part of His church was complete.

"Now, see what happens when My people reach out to each other and allow their lives to become interdependent."

And He breathed upon the newly built structure. I watched in awe as a strange, cement-like mixture flowed over the living bricks, smoothing over any tiny cracks and filling in the gaps.

"I pour in My love to make them complete, to give them strength and power and beauty," the Master explained.

Then He sat beside me and we watched in delight as people from all around gathered to find shelter, comfort and security within its walls. And the One who sat with me was also with them for the whole structure shone with the radiance of His presence. I sensed His pleasure as all at once a hymn of praise was raised to the Glorious One who was, at one and the same time, the foundation, the chief cornerstone, the great designer and the master builder of this amazing structure of living bricks.

Penitent

You were conquered,
Flesh -
Vanquished, overcome.
But then you raised your head,
And here I stand
Ashamed,
Angry at my loss of self-control.
So once again I bow the knee
To plead forgiveness from the throne.
Anxious to be clean
By washing in the blood;
Aware that Holiness must turn away from sin,
But Mercy reaches out his hand;
Forgiveness flows, is felt within
Till yet again in righteousness I stand,
So thankful that His Love remains the same.
There's no withholding of that Love
each time He sees my shame,
Instead He draws me closer by His Grace,
And lifts my eyes once more to gaze upon His face.

The Armoury

I walked despondently to where the Master stood waiting. I was tired, dirty and dishevelled. The beautiful garments He had given me were soiled and torn.

"What has happened?" He enquired.

"I was out there, outside, in the battlefield," I wearily replied, tugging vainly at a dart that remained lodged in my arm.

"The enemy defeated you?" was the next question.

I was ashamed to meet His eyes, so with head downcast, I muttered, "Yes." He said nothing for a moment and I feared the worst.

"He's going to throw me out of His House," I thought.

"Does it hurt?" He asked. There was such sympathy in His voice that I summoned up enough courage to look into His face. There I was surprised to see no condemnation, only love, compassion and sorrow. I began to cry.

"Yes, it hurts. The wounds are deep, I feel bruised all over and my spirit is broken. I thought I could fight in the battle, but the enemy is too cunning, too strong."

He touched me then, just laid His hand on my head and I was amazed to find that my wounds began to heal, my bruises faded and His peace soothed my broken spirit.

"You need some armour," He said. "Come with Me."

He walked briskly down the corridor and I limped after Him, trying to imagine myself in armour.

We came to a large iron door. It creaked gently as He pushed it open.

"My Armoury," He announced.

We had entered what appeared to be more a warehouse than a room, a huge place, filled with lines of cupboards, lockers and open shelves. On the shelves I could see rows of shoes, belts and other articles that I assumed were all pieces of armour, though some of them looked very strange indeed.

"First of all," the Master said, "I want to show you something."

He led me down one of the narrow aisles and stopped beside a mirror.

"This is my mirror of awareness. Tell me what you see," and with these words, He positioned me in front of the mirror.

"Oh how strange! However did that get there?" I asked as I put my hand to my head. It didn't feel any different but in the mirror I could clearly see that I was wearing some sort of headgear. It was well-padded, a neat fit, and covered all of my head completely. It had a visor to shield my eyes, a nose piece and a chin protector. I examined my reflection closely for a moment, then asked,

"What is it? It looks like a helmet."

"That helmet," the Master replied, "is the reason why the enemy couldn't totally defeat you today. It is called the Helmet of Salvation."

"But I don't know how it got there. I didn't know I was wearing it."

The Master smiled. "It was fitted on your head the day you walked through the Gate of My House. It doesn't come off, you will always wear it. It protects your mind from one of the enemy's firiest darts - doubt. But his doubts cannot harm you if you are aware that the Helmet of Salvation is securely strapped to your head."

"Now," He continued, "let me kit you out with the rest of your armour."

He opened one of the nearby cupboards and pulled out a strange piece of armour that resembled a half vest.

"This is the Breastplate of Righteousness. See, it matches perfectly the beautiful robe I gave you in the Robe Chamber. It will protect your robe from being soiled or torn."

It looked heavy and uncomfortable but when I put it on, I found that I was hardly aware of it at all.

"This covers your heart," said the Master, "and will keep you from sinning when the enemy fires his temptation darts."

From an open shelf labelled "Belts" He lifted a piece of armour that looked more like a girdle than a belt. He fastened it around my waist and once again, though it seemed so strong, it was light and comfortable to wear.

"My Belt of Truth," he told me as He made sure it was properly fastened, "Some of the enemy's most successful darts are lies but if you wear truth around your waist, his lies cannot hurt you."

We walked to yet another open shelf and He took down a pair of shoes so ugly that I almost refused to wear them. He laughed at my pride.

"Try them on," He urged.

With poor grace, I reached out for one of the shoes. It was made from thick leather, with heavy laces and the sole appeared to be made of brass. I eased my foot into the shoe and was amazed to find that it fitted like a glove and felt soft and pliable. Soon both shoes were on my feet and I felt like an athlete waiting for the race to begin.

"The Shoes of Readiness," the Master explained. "When you wear them, you are ready to serve Me, ready to witness for Me, ready to speak of Me. Leave them behind, and the enemy's darts of apathy and laziness will cripple you."

We walked across the huge room to the other side where row after row of great lockers stood. He opened one and took out a massive shield of burnished brass. It was beautifully engraved and shone brightly. He used the two leather straps halfway down it to fasten it to my arm. It was so big that I had to peep around the side of it to talk to Him.

"This is the Shield of Faith," He said. "There will be moments in the battle when it will seem that the enemy has singled you out for attack. He will fire darts of every description at you - difficulty, hardship, persecution, misunderstanding, fear. In those moments you mustn't panic and run defeated from the battlefield. Instead, just plant your shield firmly in the ground and hide behind it. When the enemy realizes that he cannot reach you, he will be the one to retreat. Take good care of your shield, polish it well, examine it for cracks and never leave it down in the battle."

I began to realize how foolish I had been to go into battle without His armour. I stood behind the shield and felt totally secure and utterly invincible.

"Now," said the Master, "you are well protected by your helmet, breastplate, belt, shoes and shield but there is one more item you require."

He walked across to another locker and in one swift movement, pulled out a mighty sword. I jumped back as it swished in His hand, its jewelled hilt with the blade of polished steel below, sparkling in the light.

"This is the only piece of armour that is a weapon. It is the only weapon you need in the battle outside, for that battle is not against flesh and blood but it is a spiritual battle and only a spiritual weapon will be effective."

As he placed it in my hand, He said, "Take the Sword of the Spirit, the Word of God. Use it often, use it wisely and you will discover how weak and vulnerable the enemy really is."

"Now you are ready for war. Return to the battlefield and serve me well," He commanded.

As I entered the battle once more, the darkness of the enemy's forces descended upon me and I felt the familiar, sickening anticipation of defeat rise up within me. But then I remembered how my sword had gleamed as the Master gave it to me and I took it from its sheath and flourished it at the enemy. I watched in astonishment as its blade cut a swathe of light through the darkness.

Victory was mine!

It's A Battle

It's a battle -
The enemy stands
Tall and defiant,
Snarling and sneering,
Gloating over our weaknesses
Triumphant when we fail,
Shouting his accusations,
Whispering his lies,
Seeking to confuse,
Distort, dishonour,
To dim the light
To quench the flame
To steal the glory.

It's a battle -
True, but listen -
It's a battle
That's been won.
So take up arms,
Resist, stand firm,
Confident of victory.
We have the armour
We have the sword
We know the Name!

And in His Name we fight,
This ground we claim,
Till darkness yields to light
And courage covers shame.
We'll wield His sword with joy,
Declare His power, His might,
Till Jesus' Name is lifted high
And Satan's put to flight.

...I just jumped right into the fountain and immersed myself in His Mercy...

The Storehouse

I walked anxiously into the corridor that would lead me to His Storehouse and was surprised to find that I had to join a long queue, stretching from its door almost to the corner where I stood. I spoke to the gentleman in front of me,
"I didn't think there would be so many people going to the Storehouse."
"Oh this is such a busy place," he told me, "I came yesterday at six o'clock in the morning and there was a queue even then."
As I prepared to wait, I looked ahead to see the huge room at the end of the corridor. In some ways, it reminded me of a barn, tall and wide and of a plain construction. The door reinforced this perception for it was a solid, heavy door on steel runners.
We had moved much closer to the door by now and the man beside me began to chat.
"Why have you come to the Storehouse?" he asked.
His question brought back my earlier anxiety.
"I'm rather afraid that my waiting may be in vain," I began. "I know that I've heard wonderful stories about the Storehouse but I'm not sure if what I need will be there - there may not be any left."
"You see, the Master asked me to undertake a task for Him, a difficult task. I have kept putting it off because I didn't have the

courage to tackle it. I'm so afraid that His patience has run out. I've come to see if He has any left in His Storehouse."

The man beside me gave me a rueful look.

"I think that you have more chance of finding what you need than I have."

As he spoke, I could hear the regret in his voice and when I looked in his face, I could see a mixture of fear and desperate longing.

"I did something wrong yesterday. I knew the moment it happened that I had sinned against the Father. I was so ashamed but I couldn't undo it. The guilt I felt kept me awake all night, tossing and turning. I won't be able to rest until I see if He will grant me some of the mercy in His Storehouse."

His voice shook and he took a deep breath to steady the intensity of his emotion.

"I don't deserve His mercy and it won't surprise me if I'm turned away."

I tried to reassure him by telling him of the many people I had met in the Master's House who had been able to obtain everything they needed from the Storehouse.

"I have never met anyone who came away emptyhanded," I encouraged him.

By this time we had reached the door and there we parted company. My friend went off to search for Mercy and I stood for a moment in the doorway. The Storehouse was even more immense than I had imagined and seemed to go on for ever into the distance. The walls were lined with barrels and sacks and crates of all sizes and shapes. The sacks were piled high to the ceiling, the crates were all neatly stacked and the barrels were lined up in orderly rows.

I heard a now familiar voice ask, "What can I do for you?" and turned to greet the Master.

I confessed to Him my situation and rather tentatively enquired if He had any Patience left.

"You only have to ask," He assured me with a smile and made His way to one of the crates nearby. I followed Him to where the huge crates were stacked and realised that everyone of them, as far as the eye could see, had Patience stamped on the side in bold, black letters. I began to smile as I realised how foolish I had been to imagine that the Master might ever run out of Patience.

"It is part of My nature," He said, "to be long-suffering or patient. What you see here is only a week's supply. I have endless quantities of Patience to give to My people. You can keep coming back for more."

As He spoke, He reached into the crate and handed to me a packet of Patience. I turned to go but he called me back.

"Don't you want anything else? Is that all you are going to ask for?"

"Well, I had wondered.........." I replied, "but I didn't want to seem greedy. Could I also have a little Grace?"

The Master shook His head and said, "I'm afraid I don't keep that in the Storehouse."

My face fell for a moment then I heard Him laugh as He continued,

"We don't keep a little Grace - we only keep lavish Grace."

He led me halfway down the huge Storehouse to where large, bulging sacks were piled to the roof.

"Take as much as you can carry. My lavish Grace is freely given. The Father delights to bestow His Grace on the children in His House. It is a wonderful commodity, useful in all sorts of situations. You'll find Grace is sufficient for sorrow, for trials, for illness, for disability, for persecution, for broken hearts and broken homes and broken promises. There's healing and strength in the Father's Grace."

The Master's generosity encouraged me to make another request.

"Can I ask for something for a friend?" I enquired. He nodded, so I explained.

"I have a friend who is mourning the loss of a loved one. Someone told me that the oil of joy can be given for mourning and I wondered if I could take some from Your Storehouse for her?"

He led me to where I had seen large barrels stored. Bright red, foot-high letters on each barrel proclaimed that here was Joy, lots of Joy! From a shelf nearby, the Master took a bottle which he filled from an open barrel.

"Give your friend a few drops of the oil of Joy, now and again, as you see the need. It might take a little while but you will see an improvement. And tell your friend to come to My Storehouse herself - there is so much here that will help."

I made my way back down the massive room to the doorway, dragging my huge sack of Grace behind me and holding tightly to the packet of Patience and the precious bottle of the oil of Joy.

As I walked through the door I heard someone call out to me and turned to see my friend from the queue, running towards me with a wide smile on his face. I was rather concerned to see that his clothes were dripping wet.

"Whatever happened to you?" I asked. "You're soaked."

"Oh, it was wonderful," he laughed. "Did you notice the fountain in the Storehouse? That is His Mercy - always flowing in an endless stream. When I asked for His Mercy, He brought me to the fountain and I was so excited to see how freely His Mercy flowed that I just jumped right into the fountain and immersed myself in His Mercy. I swam in it, splashed in it, poured it over my head. I felt His Mercy cleanse my guilt until it had all gone. Oh, it is so wonderful.........."

and still laughing, he ran off down the corridor.

I smiled at his enthusiasm, glad that he had found such abundant mercy. What an amazing place His Storehouse had turned out to be. I looked once more at the riches bestowed upon me with such extravagance and I vowed to return again and again to partake of its bounties.

Something More

You think you have come to the end,
But there'll always be something more,
Delights unimagined, joys never known
In the Father's bounteous store.

You think you have poured out the oil,
Exhausted the flour in the sack,
You feel that you've used up His blessings
But the Father keeps giving them back.

You think you have mined all the riches,
That you're holding the last of His treasure,
But your Father's a God of abundance
Who gives gems to His own without measure.

So receive what He gives you with gladness,
Come again and again to His store,
God delights to lavish His blessing,
There will always be something more.

On a few occasions in recent years, it has been my joy to take part in a "Quiet Day", a day spent by a group of women in silence (not an easy task for some of us!) We devote the day to prayer, meditation, reading or whatever we feel God is calling us to do.

The Quiet Day at which "Picnic in the Valley" was written was an unusually warm October Saturday in 1997. The views from the house were stunning, overlooking the bay where the famous Mountains of Mourne "sweep down to the sea". The garden was beautifully kept and featured a little stream which flowed down one side of the house. We had been encouraged to meditate on the twenty-third Psalm and as I thought of the words, "Thou preparest a table before me", I began to feel as though the Master Himself had provided yet another special time for me, a picnic in the valley.

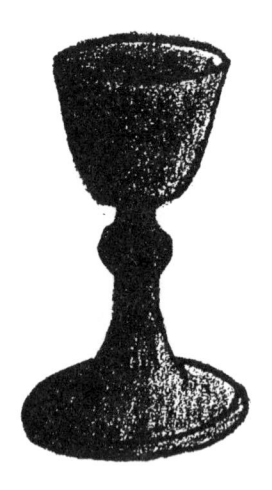

... still the cup of joy ran over ...

Picnic in the Valley

I walked the valley and the mist hung low over the hills on either side. My enemy was never far behind and as I walked I felt his darts - fatigue, pressure, busyness, laziness, emptiness. Each one slowed me down until it felt that I might be compelled to stay in this valley forever. My leaden feet could never again carry me to the top of the mountain where I knew the sun shone in splendour and His glory stretched into infinity.

Then at the lowest point in the valley, a gentle touch alerted me to His presence. He drew me from the wooded path where I had been walking into a clearing near the river. Wearily I took a seat on a tree stump and listened for a moment to the song the river sang, a song of peace and things eternal.

As the song began to quieten my spirit, I sensed that in the trees beyond, my enemies were gathering to renew their attack, but with a single gesture of authority, the Shepherd bade them cease. Then, in the presence of my enemies, He laid a table, a picnic by the river. A cloth of purest white was spread and while the river sweetly sang its song, He placed upon the cloth His gifts to me - His rest, His strength. He waited patiently by my side while I fed hungrily from His table and His quiet presence soothed me like a balm.

Then on the cloth before me, He gently placed a cup - my cup, fashioned specially for me, engraved with my name. He began to pour into my cup the sparkling wine of His joy. He poured until the cup was filled right to the brim, but didn't stop and soon the golden liquid overflowed, running down the sides of the cup in a joyous, bubbling stream. I watched as it spread on the cloth, flowed over the edges of the table and dripped on the grass at my feet. I smiled, then laughed aloud in sheer delight at what I saw. I looked into His face and saw that He was laughing too.

I leaned forward to drink from the cup and soon my emptiness was filled up with His joy and even as I drank, the Shepherd poured and kept on pouring and still the cup of joy ran over and still we laughed, my God and I together at His table.

And all around I knew my enemies watched in helpless silence: bound, ineffective by His presence. In that moment, I knew there would be other valleys up ahead but never again need the mist on the hills depress me or the darts of the enemy discourage me. I would always hold the memory of the picnic and in other valleys I would see His table spread, His laughing eyes, His joy poured out and overflowing.

The God Who ...

He's the God who is the Lord of all creation,
The God whose Word brought forth the stars and sun,
Whose hand controls the orbit of the planets,
He is the Sovereign Lord, the great, Almighty One.

He's the God who condescends to walk before me,
Who leads me to a quiet place to rest,
Who finds the greenest pasture for my feeding,
The path He chooses always is the best.

He's the God who's always there, no matter what,
Whose rod and staff bring comfort in my pain,
And even in the darkness of the valley,
Awareness of His presence gives me hope again.

He's the God who makes provision for my need,
Invites me to His table, prepares it just for me.
Fills up my cup with joy that's overflowing,
Pours out His love and care so lavishly.

He's the God whom I shall see in all His splendour,
And in whose House I'll dwell for evermore,
Whose glories I shall gaze on through the ages,
Join Heaven's angels as they worship and adore.

... they'll call my Son a rose - sweet rose of Sharon ...

The Rose

We walked slowly and contentedly out of the valley and approached the House through the gardens. The rosebeds were in full bloom and I reached down to pick one of the beautiful yellow roses, then exclaimed loudly as the sharp thorns pricked my fingers.

"Ouch! Why do such beautiful flowers have such awful thorns?" I cried.

"Sit down for a moment," the Master suggested. "Enjoy the fragrance and the beauty while I tell you a story. We'll call it 'The Rose'.

In the days of Creation, the Father desired to place something in His world that would speak of Himself. But what would it be? Perhaps a flower.......

He began with a slender stem from which would grow leaves of darkest green. The tops of the leaves He brushed with a coating of satin, so smooth and silky, then delicately cut a fine pattern into the edges. The care He took to shape each leaf and to mark it with its intricate edging spoke of the care He takes to shape lives and mark them with His own hand.

The tiny veins within each leaf would feed the sunlight to His flower and as long as the leaf held up its shiny surface to the light, energy would pour in. This would remind His people to stay in His light, absorbing all the amazing provision of life and energy and strength available from His bountiful supplies.

Then the Father began to shape a bud. He searched His vast kingdom for the softest petals, silky, velvety to touch, then selected from His palette the most beautiful array of colours, carefully dipping the petals in palest pink, brightest yellow, purest white or darkest red. The petals He then packed inside each bud till no hint of colour could be seen. Each petal had been arranged in exactly the right position, overlapping a little, touching here and there in just the right places, firmly held together at the base.

"Now," He said, "when each bud opens and the petals unfurl, they will form a flower of such beauty that something within the hearts of my people will rise up in response. Lovers will use this flower to say 'I love you', brides will carry it to express their joy and those who mourn will present it as an act of sympathy. It will adorn palaces and great halls and will inspire poetry and songs."

"The tiny bud will surely tell my people that in each new believer, though it may not be seen at first, there is such potential for beauty, the beauty of a life slowly unfurling under My tender care".

He gave His flower a name - the rose - and knew its beauty would speak of His beauty, the splendour of His holiness and righteousness and purity. Then, deep within the heart of every petal of every rose, He placed a tiny drop of perfume.

"I'm giving this flower a special fragrance," He said, "to remind My children of the sweetness of My presence. They will know My fragrance as they draw closer to Me in intimate fellowship and, as the scent of the rose lingers in a room, so My people will be known by the fragrance of My Son, for their lives will touch the lives of others and they too will experience something of His sweetness."

He picked up a now perfectly formed rose and looked thoughtfully at the smooth stem.

"This rose is not complete - something else is needed."

And all along the stem, He began to fashion thorns, with sharp points that hurt and wounded.

"My people need to know." He said, "that beauty is often marred by ugliness, that joy is often accompanied by sorrow, that success and failure are close companions, that hope sometimes gives way to despair, that love may turn to hatred. But when they gaze on a rose,

I want them to remember that the sharpness of the thorns are very close to the softness of the petals. I want those who are wounded by the thorns of life to take comfort from the sweetness of the fragrance that lingers just above the thorns. For I am always there when the sharp prick is felt and the heart begins to bleed. And I want them to remember Someone else who wore a crown of thorns on their behalf, who knows their sorrow for He felt it too, whose beauty was marred, whose mission seemed to fail and whose love was thrown back in His face. Let the thorns remind them that He walked the road they walk, so He knows the best way through."

He touched a petal with a gentle hand,

"They'll call My Son a rose," He said, "Sweet Rose of Sharon".

Store Up Beauty

Store up beauty to remember
When days are dull and grey,
Store up memories of peace and calm
To hold the hounds of war at bay.

Store up the fragrance of a rose
To make another day smell sweet,
Store up the softness of the sand
For times when sharp rocks cut your feet.

Store up the singing of a bird
For times when songs aren't heard to play,
Keep the music of the water
For a sad and silent day.

Store up mem'ries of God's kindness
To turn man's cruelty away,
Keep recollections of His love
For times when hatred has its say.

Store up the faithfulness of God
For seasons when He hides His face,
Recollect the joy He gave
When all you know is grief's embrace.

Store up His beauty to remember
When your life is dull and grey,
Store up His grace and tender mercy
To ponder over every day.

My prayer partner, Lavinia, is particularly fond of a verse in Psalm 139, which says,
"*All the days ordained for me were written in Your book before one of them came to be.*"
When our days are difficult, it is of immense comfort to remember that God has prior knowledge of them and so can supply the strength and the grace we need to endure them. It is our choice, of course, whether we live those days in joyful acceptance or in bitter resentment.

The Library

I was tired from walking in the valley so I was greatly relieved when the Master said, "I know where you can rest," and he added with a twinkle in His kindly eyes, "I think this will turn out to be one of your favourite rooms."

By this time we had reached a beautifully carved double door which the Master flung open with a flourish.

"My Library," He announced.

The room was high ceilinged, its walls lined with bookcases made from the finest mahogany. Scattered here and there were well-lit desks and comfortable chairs, while in an elegantly curtained bay window, I could see a padded, cushioned armchair and footstool into which I sank gratefully. The view from the window was magnificent - high mountains and the river flowing through the valley from which I had just returned.

The atmosphere was calm and quiet and the air smelt of leather and ink, printing presses and new paper. This was a room in which I could not only rest, but also read and study and write.

Feeling suddenly invigorated, I jumped up to examine the bookshelves. The Master came with me and smiled indulgently as I ran from bookcase to bookcase, exclaiming at the titles of the books. This was no ordinary library. These were no ordinary books.

One entire wall was covered with books classified under the title 'Great Lives'. Here I found Moses, Paul, Rebecca, Mary, David, Isaiah.

"May I read these books?" I asked. "I've so longed to know what happened on Mount Sinai when Moses met with God and I've always been so curious about what it was really like for Mary to rear the young Jesus. It must have been so wonderful."

The Master laughed at my excitement. "Of course you can read these books - that's why they're here."

Another bookcase caught my eye. Carved in the wood above the door were the words 'Great Mysteries Explained'. I ran my eye along the titles - 'Ezekiel's Wheels within Wheels', 'Daniel's Strange Beasts', 'Revelation's Horsemen', 'Creation'.

"Oh, I've often wondered about these things. All the answers are here? For me to read?" I asked, scarcely able to accept the implications of what I saw.

"All that and so much more," came the Master's quiet voice. He motioned to another set of books, bearing as a title the single word 'Truth'.

"My people don't always understand My Word, the one book I sent to earth." He continued, and I could hear a tone of sadness in His voice, "They argue about their interpretations of it. They fall out when they can't agree. But here is truth - the truth about election, sanctification, the gifts of the Holy Spirit."

"So much to learn," I breathed in awe. "Must I leave this room? Can I not just stay here?" I pleaded.

"Now child, have patience," He replied. "There is no rush, no time limit. You have all of eternity to assimilate the knowledge that is here. I'm going to leave you in this quiet place for a while, but first I want to show you two special books."

He went to a shelf and from it took a heavy book, richly bound in beautifully embossed leather. It was old, as old as time itself and its title gleamed in letters of pure gold, 'The Lamb's Book of Life.'

He carefully opened the book and ran His finger down the page. "Look," He said, and there I saw my name and beside it a date, 23rd April 1961. I looked at Him with tears in my eyes.

"Yes," He said, "the date on which you knelt at my cross."

"But will my name always be there?" I asked, suddenly afraid that someone or something might cause my name to be removed.

"Don't be alarmed," He reassured me, "no one can eradicate your name from My Book of Life. Nothing will ever cause the ink even to fade. When I met you at the cross, I wrote your name Myself."

"And the other book?" I enquired.

"Ah, My Book of Days," the Master said, as He crossed once more to the bookshelves and lifted down another volume.

"This is the book you are writing." I spun round, shocked by what He had said.

"The book I'm writing? No, I'm not writing any book," I protested.

The Master silenced my protests with a smile.

"The days I have ordained for you are all written here, but I have given you certain choices about how you fill those days. What you live is what is written." With those words, He led me to the armchair at the window and left the room.

I lay back in the chair to rest and His words were ringing in my ears,

"What you live is what is written."

And I wondered what sort of book I was writing, and whether, as He wrote my days in His Book, He did so with joy or sadness. I vowed from that time on to give Him good days to record, days of joyful service, thankful praise and heartfelt worship.

Mary and Martha

Martha opened up her home to Him.
She heard, with great excitement,
That He was on His way to Bethany.
"We'll have Him here - He'll need to rest,
We'll give a feast for Him - our very best."

She got up early - made the bread,
Talked Lazarus into giving her a lamb,
Borrowed extra bowls and little stools,
Went to the market - bought the fish,
And made for Him her most exotic dish.

"He's here," the cry went up, "the Lord is here."
And Martha rushed to welcome all her friends,
Bring them to the courtyard at the back,
Make sure all twelve disciples had a seat,
And bring the bowl and towels for their feet.

She flew outside to stir the cooking pot,
Filled to the brim the empty waterjars,
Smelt the fragrance of the roasting lamb,
And thought, "The Master will enjoy this treat,"
Then caught sight of Mary, sitting idle at His feet.

"Well - isn't that just typical -
Sixteen for dinner and she's just sitting there!
She knows I need some help to serve the meal,
And surely Jesus knows - He doesn't seem to care."

Resentment grew in Martha's heart -
She ran to Jesus without another thought,
"Master, Mary should be helping me,
Tell her, Jesus, tell her that she ought."

Jesus looked at Martha, gently smiled,
He saw beneath the anger, Martha's loving heart,
And simply said to her in mild rebuke,
"Your sister Mary chose the better part."

But late that night, when all had gone to rest,
Martha sat, reflecting on her day,
She'd served her Lord a meal and washed His feet,
But couldn't bring to mind one thing He had to say.

She listened then to Mary, as she spoke
Of all the joy and wonder of His Word,
And how her spirit burned within her,
As she worshipped and adored her Lord.

There was another feast, another time,
When Mary poured her precious ointment on His feet,
And Martha served, this time without rebuke,
For Martha, as she served, was bathed in fragrance sweet.

The Mary in me needs to sit at Jesus' feet,
Pour out my heart to Him in worship and in praise,
Nestle close to feel His comfort and His love,
Listen carefully to what the Master says.

My Martha has to learn to serve without rebuke
Give gladly of my time and of my love,
Working hard, yet covered in His perfume sweet,
Pausing now and then to worship God above.

May my worship
Permeate my work.

Two of the images in 'The Waiting Room' have their inspiration in my family. The section which tells of the saint's passage into the glory of Heaven was written the morning after my father died, a few years ago. As I stood at his bedside in his last hours, the Lord gave me the lovely picture of the royal barge being prepared to carry His child over the troubled water. I will always be grateful to God for giving me the courage to read the passage at my father's funeral. Bereavement is a hard part of the journey but if we allow Him, God can meet us in a special way even as we mourn.

The image of the frail old lady who looked eagerly for death is based directly on my mother-in-law. Granny Kearney is ninety-seven years old and many of those ninety-seven years have been spent in the service of the King, at home and also abroad as a missionary. For the past few years, she has been anxious to "go home".
The sincerity of her desire can be judged by the little story which often makes us smile:

Our church has a reputation for prayer and has seen many remarkable answers to prayer. Granny must have been reflecting on this one day because she turned to her son, Robert and said,

"I hope the people in the church aren't praying for me to get better!"

The Waiting Room

I had spent a wonderful evening with the Master, walking in His garden, enjoying the splendour of the setting sun, talking together in the closeness of the fellowship that hardly needed words.

"Come," He said suddenly, "I want to show you a rather special room."

Once indoors, He led me to a door on which I could read the words 'Waiting Room'. I stopped and backed away from the door.

"What's the matter?" the Master enquired.

"It's the name - I've never liked waiting rooms - they remind me of dentists and doctors and draughty railway stations."

"Well," He smiled, "I think you will find My Waiting Room a pleasant surprise. Don't be afraid. Go on in."

Somewhat timidly, I pushed the door open and peered inside. It was a room full of people, cheerfully chatting together, some resting comfortably on the huge sofas that took up most of the floor space. It was decorated in the colours of the sky, the deep midnight blue of the carpet contrasting with the bright summer blue of the walls. As I looked around I realized that it was a room full of light, streaming in from the immense picture window that took up one entire wall. There was a buzz in the atmosphere - a buzz of excitement, of anticipation.

I turned to the Master. "I don't understand. What is the purpose of this room? What are they all waiting for?"

"Why don't you go and talk to some of them?" He suggested.

Still feeling rather apprehensive, I looked around for someone with whom I might be comfortable conversing. In a nearby corner, I spotted a young lady sitting quietly on her own. I asked her what she was doing in the room.

"I'm waiting patiently," she replied calmly, "just as the Master advised."

I looked puzzled so she went on to explain.

"I was faced with a very difficult situation in my life and I didn't know which way to turn. I couldn't make any sense of what the Master was doing in it all so He advised me to simply come to this room and wait patiently. I know now that He will show me what to do in His own time."

Being somewhat reassured by this encounter, I plucked up the courage to approach a group of people who were talking animatedly at a table in the centre of the room.

"Excuse me, can you tell me why you are here?" I asked and with one voice came the reply,

"We're waiting for His coming!"

All but one white-haired gentleman returned excitedly to their discussion, gesticulating across the table, arguing heatedly the merits of various points of view, looking up reference books to confirm their opinions. I looked in bewilderment at the one person who seemed willing to talk to me. He smiled in some amusement at His friends.

"Don't let them frighten you," He said, "they get a bit excited about it sometimes. You see, the Master has planned a great dramatic return to earth. We don't know when it will be, we don't know many details about it but we're waiting."

His face lit up with eager anticipation, "This must be the most exciting room in the house. Every day we find new reason to believe that His coming will be soon. Just imagine the scene - the King of Heaven returning in clouds of glory, triumphant and victorious, in full view of all who are on the earth. What a picture!"

I felt my heart rise in response to his enthusiasm as I moved on to a frail old lady who sat huddled in a big armchair, her head leaning on the wing of the chair, her eyes closed. She looked up as I drew near and invited me to sit down.

"Tell me," I asked, "what are you waiting for?"

"Why, child," she replied with a twinkle in her eye, "I'm just waiting to go home. I'm tired of living in this part of His House. It's only temporary, you know, and I'm going to get a new body in my new home. This one is really worn out, full of aches and pains and I'm so looking forward to my new one."

She gave a little sigh and whispered, "I do wish the Master would hurry up."

I found it quite disturbing that she could talk of death in these terms so I went to ask the Master about it.

"How can she be so calm? Surely no one looks forward to death. The whole idea scares me. Oh I just knew I wouldn't like this room!"

The Master took me by the arm and gently led me to the large picture window.

"I know that you are afraid of death but really there is no need for you to be. As the old lady says - it is just like going home. I think the time has come for you to witness a homecoming."

"Oh, please, no," I begged, "I don't think I would like that at all."

"It won't be easy," He agreed, "But I will stand right beside you and you can lean on me for strength and comfort. You need to do this, child, so that you need never fear death again. Now, just stand at the window and watch."

As I looked out, I began to realize that I was gazing into the vastness of eternity. As I watched, a picture slowly formed until I could perceive a river and in my spirit I knew it was the river of death. I shrank from what I saw but the Master put His arm around me to encourage me. Then I noticed a figure standing on the near river bank.

"One of My saints," said the Master. "Watch closely."

The saint stood at the water's edge. Before him stretched a long expanse, beyond which he could perceive the hazy outline of the Heavenly City. But how was he to cross the river? The water was rough, the waves high - it seemed too difficult a task.

On the other shore the angels put the finishing touches to a wonderful mansion and soon the word was passed along:

"He's there - at the water's edge. The saint is on his way."

One watchful angel cried out in concern:

"But see the river - it is rough today. The waves are too high for him to cross."

"No need to worry," said another, "The King has sent word to prepare the royal barge."

Soon there was great activity as the angels made ready the royal barge, lining it with silken pillows of peace, comfort and gentleness, then, with a little push, sending it to the very place where the saint stood waiting.

He stepped in, lay down in calm serenity, and then a gentle breeze drove the barge out into the river. And as he crossed, the prayers and thoughts of those who watched from the bank enfolded the barge as it forged a path through the waves.

"The God of Jacob is my refuge. God is my strength and my song. He has become my salvation. My peace I give unto you."

The barge slipped quietly into its mooring at Heaven's gate and the saint stepped out into radiant light, trumpets sounding, angels singing. They lined the path as he made his way to the throne and there, with a gesture of utmost delight, laid his crown at his Saviour's feet.

The saint was home.

I turned to the Master with the tears running down my face. He understood my tears.

"Yes," He said, "it is both sad and beautiful - so sad for you but so beautiful for him. You will stand there one day but I will be with you even as you cross the river. There is nothing to fear."

I had walked with the Master through His House and he had always been at my side. I knew now that when I entered His Waiting Room for the final time, I could do so with gladness, knowing that its exit would lead to the glories of a new home in Heaven, the wonders of an eternity spent in worship and praise and the inexpressible joy of seeing my wonderful Master face to face, with no veil between us to hide His splendour and His majesty.

Words of Love

You whispered words of love to me,
Filled my soul with ecstasy,
I didn't know You loved me so.
I could hardly take it in,
That in spite of all my sin,
Such sweet tenderness You would bestow.

"You are a much-loved and cherished one,
I gave Jesus, my only Son,
To show you that I love you so.
I'm delighted with you,
Every day my love is new,
I'll reveal my heart for you to know."

I want to capture the moment,
Hold it forever,
And let nothing take it away.
May my heart hold Your words,
Your expression of love,
May they fill me with joy every day.

SECTION TWO
Healing Rooms

The Emergency Room

The Examination Room

Visitors

The Operating Room

Isolation Ward

Opthalmics

Maternity Ward

Psalm 107 vs 19-22

They cried to the Lord in their trouble, and He saved them from their distress. He sent forth His word and healed them; he rescued them from the grave.

Let them give thanks to the Lord for His unfailing love and His wonderful deeds for men.

Let them sacrifice thank-offerings and tell of His works with songs of joy.

I had spent the day at an English Agreement Trial, looking at pieces of coursework submitted by various pupils, in an attempt to ensure that the standard of marking by English teachers would be as uniform as possible. All day I had been slightly bothered by a pain in my side and as I approached the Health Centre on my way home, I decided to call in and have it checked out. The doctor was busy and I turned away, saying that I wouldn't bother waiting but the receptionist persuaded me to sit for a moment or two. When the doctor examined me, he was more concerned than I was and told me he wanted me to go to hospital.

"Could it not wait until tomorrow?" I asked.

"No," was the reply.

"Well, is it all right if I just drive myself over to the hospital?"

"No, I'd be happier if you got someone else to drive you there."

So my poor brother-in-law, who had just that day arrived over from England for a visit, was greeted by a pale face and a doctor's letter and the request,

"Do you mind driving me to Casualty?"

Later that night my inflamed appendix was removed by a young surgeon who had earlier delivered the ultimate insult by telling me that I was "really too old to have appendicitis"!

It would be difficult to anticipate how an operation to remove an appendix could possibly result in any special moments but the whole concept for this section entitled 'Healing Rooms' was born out of that experience. It all took place just before Christmas (the worst possible time in a Music teacher's calendar!) but the days of convalesence provided an oasis of calm in a busy life that resulted in a burst of creative activity, providing so many special moments along the way that it is hard to remember them all.

We all have been wounded in some way, at some time, by the enemy or even by our friends but God does provide a place of healing. May you experience the soothing balm of His presence and love as you walk with me through His 'Healing Rooms'.

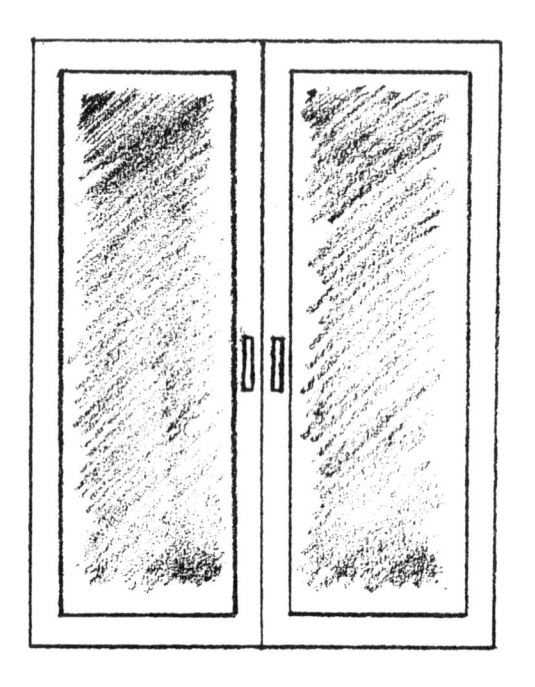

... *the door opens wide to receive you* ...

The Emergency Room

I leaned heavily on the Master's arm as I limped painfully up the path. In the fierce heat of the battle, I had allowed my shield of Faith to slip and the fiery dart of the enemy had found its target. I had been wounded.

As I lay in pain and distress, while the noise and chaos of war waged all around me, the Master came to me. Without a word He gave me His hand and half-led, half-carried me to a wing in His House that I had never visited and to the door before which I now stood.

It was a wide, ceiling-high automatic door, emblazoned with large, red letters, spelling out the words "Emergency Room". As we approached, it slid open to allow us to enter.

"Oh, I'm so glad it opened like that," I sighed, "I don't think I would have the strength to open an ordinary door."

"I designed it so for that very reason. Many of the people who come to this room are so badly hurt that having a door to block their way would just be the final straw. You have only to approach My Emergency Room and the door opens wide to receive you."

I eased myself onto a chair and prepared to wait for someone to attend to me. I tried to position my leg so that the wound throbbed less painfully, then began to look around.

This was a bustling, noisy place but the bustling was not that of frenzy or chaos. Instead it had an air of order, purpose and efficiency. Words were not wasted on the triviality of small talk, decisions were made without panic or fuss. I was aware that this was a place of security, a place where my pain and suffering would surely be alleviated.

All around me were the sounds of people in distress - a heavy sigh from the white-faced man behind me; a stifled moan from the lady in the opposite chair; the sobs of a young girl in the far corner, as she leaned against the one sitting beside her.

I turned to the Master. "So many hurting people. Did they all get wounded in the battle?"

He looked around for a moment, then replied, "Many of them have been wounded as you were. The enemy never misses an opportunity to attack and he's so good at finding the smallest chink in the armour. He targets My soldiers where they are most vulnerable and in a split second his dart has found its mark."

I lifted my face to look into His as I listened.

"Oh Master," I breathed, "There are others then, like me? I thought I was the only one to fall, to bring disgrace to You. I was so ashamed."

He smiled and in His smile was forgiveness and understanding.

"Don't worry, child," He said, "I know how hard it is to be on your guard all the time."

He paused for a moment, then gestured to some patients sitting near the door.

"Not all are here because of the battle," He said and as He spoke, I could hear the disappointment in His tone.

"These pale, languid ones came to My House some years ago but they don't want to fight in the battle. Their whole desire is to sit by the river in the sunshine or feast at My table in the Banqueting Hall. I gave them My armour but they have allowed it to become dull and rusty through disuse."

"So why are they here?" I asked.

"Well," replied the Master, sadly, "they have contracted a disease called Apathy and now they are dismayed to find that when they try to walk, their limbs are stiff and sore and when they try to eat the delicacies from My table, they are sick."

I found it hard to imagine anyone not wanting to serve this wonderful Master who had walked with me for so many years.

"How terrible," I said, "can they be cured?"

"They can if they want to be," was His reply, "but sometimes the disease spreads so quickly that even the desire to be healed is lost."

Just then a nurse came to attend to my injury. She smiled at the Master as though she knew Him well and began to examine my leg.

"Let's go to an Examination Room. We'll treat you there," she suggested and began to help me to my feet.

I turned quickly to the Master.

"Please, before we go, just tell me one thing. You have been with me from the moment I was wounded. What about all these other people? Why are you not with them? Don't they need you as much as I do?"

The nurse and the Master exchanged knowing glances then He very gently admonished me.

"Ah child, how could you think that I could let any of My children suffer alone? I am with them too. You may not always be aware of Me when you look at hurting people, but I'm there. You see the young girl crying on her friend's shoulder? I'm there, in that friend - her arms are My arms to bring comfort and support."

As I hobbled out of the Emergency Room, I looked back at all the wounded, distressed people and my heart sang as I realized afresh the wonder of His omnipresence. As He had been with me, helping me to bear my pain, encouraging me to lean on Him for support, whispering comfort in my ear when my strength failed, so at the same time and in the same measure, He could pour out His grace and His compassion on all who knew pain and suffering to be their portion. And I breathed a prayer of thanksgiving that however freely His grace was poured out, it would never be diminished, it would never run out, but would flow for ever in a constant, healing stream from the throne of the Father.

Apathy

It began with being tired,
Too weary to be of use,
Next time I wasn't really tired -
Just used it for my excuse.

Embarrassment set in,
How could I go back there?
I thought I'd be conspicuous,
That everyone would stare.

The less I was involved,
The less I seemed to care,
And soon my feet were trapped
In Satan's wily snare.

When Apathy took over,
I needed no excuse -
I could no more be bothered,
And I ceased to be of use!

The Examination Room

The Examination Room was tiny and at first sight contained only an examination table, a sink and a chair. The nurse helped me on to the table and as I lay back and looked around me, I became aware that the room also contained a large light, a bright light that could bend and twist in every direction.

The light hurt my eyes and I shrank from it, painfully aware that the wound, of which I was already ashamed, seemed more ugly as the light shone above it.

The Master came to stand at my side and His words explained the strange feeling of shame that threatened to overwhelm me,

"That is the light of My Holiness. My people are always examined in its light. Don't shrink from it - welcome it rather, for in its light, I can assess the full extent of your injury and the damage done to bone and tissue can be revealed."

He explored my wound with gentle fingers and I waited anxiously for the verdict.

"The wound is very deep," He said, and I was comforted by the compassion in His voice.

"It needs to be stitched together firmly by My Word and encircled in the bandage of My Love. I want you to rest from the battle for a while, until it heals. We will keep you here and My staff will care lovingly for you as you regain your strength."

"Thank you Master," I said with some relief. "I know I don't deserve Your tenderness and compassion. But what will happen when I return to the battle? What if my shield slips again?"

I became quite agitated at the memory of the battle and the pain of the enemy's dart and the disgrace I felt as I lay wounded and helpless. He reached out to touch my hand and immediately His touch soothed me and quietened my agitation.

"While you rest," He assured me, "I have prescribed for you some medicine to strengthen your faith. Take it regularly, finish the course, and when you return to the battle, you will find your shield of faith has grown larger and stronger. It will not slip so easily."

"And what is this medicine?" I asked.

"Its name is Promise. My word is full of wonderful promises, faith-building promises. Just listen for a moment."

His voice grew tender as He fixed His eyes on my face and softly whispered His promises to me:

"I will never leave you or forsake you............
   I will turn the desert into pools of water...............
I have covered you with the shadow of My hand............
   I will sustain you and I will rescue you............
I will uphold you with My righteous, right hand............"

A tear trickled down my cheek as I listened to His words. Faith rose up within me and I made a firm resolve to know more of His promises and to learn to rely on them.

The Master continued, "Don't waste this time when you are set aside from service but use it wisely. The enemy meant this to harm you, to cause disillusionment and defeat in your life but, if you allow Me, I can turn it into good, into something that will strengthen you, into something that will ultimately help you to gain victory in the battle."

Promises

The God who never lies,
Whose word is yea or nay,
Always can be trusted
Keeps His promise, come what may.

He never breaks His Word
And what He says is true.
And I perceive each day reveals
His faithfulness anew.

So I can rest upon His Word,
Each time He says "I will........"
Allow His many promises
My heart and mind to fill.

When Satan taunts, I will not fear,
I'll cry out to my Lord,
Lay down a promise giv'n to me,
Stand firmly on His Word.

... the beautiful aroma spread through the whole ward ...

Visitors

As visiting time approached, I became very excited. Now that I was feeling a little better, I was looking forward to having some company and spending time chatting to my friends. I wondered who would come, what they would say to me and even what they might bring to cheer me up!

My first visitor arrived early - an old friend who was going through a difficult time herself. I was pleased to see her as I was sure that she would understand just how I felt and be able to offer the comfort that I needed. She was carrying a large box which she placed on top of me, over my heart, and then she sat at my bedside and chatted to me for a long time. As I listened to her, I became more and more puzzled, because her gift got heavier and heavier as each moment passed. I didn't like to complain in case I offended her but, by the time she left, I was feeling quite uncomfortable. I opened the box and peered inside and all at once I understood what had happened. My friend had brought her own heavy burden to me and laid it on my heart.

I was too weak to lift her burden off my heart and lay there wondering what to do when I heard another footstep approach my bed. I was greatly relieved to see that my next visitor was a tall, strong man.

"Oh please," I begged, "can you remove this burden? It is too heavy for me to hold."

He quickly reached out, lifted the burden in his strong arms and set it aside.

"I hope my present won't cause you so much distress," he said with a smile, placing on the bed beside me a brightly wrapped candy box, tied with a cheerful, multi-coloured bow. I opened it eagerly and gasped with delight at what I saw.

"I called in to the Master's Kitchen this morning, " explained my friend, "and He gave me a box of Encouragement sweetmeats for you. I hope you like them."

"The Master always knows what I need," I replied. "These are just wonderful!"

I sampled one of the sweetmeats and it tasted like the sweetest honey. As I ate, the words of encouragement lifted my downcast spirit and I thanked my visitor over and over again for taking the trouble to go to the Master's Kitchen on my behalf.

A little later, another friend arrived, a busy lady, whom I had not expected to see. We had a pleasant time together, then just before she turned to leave, she began to apologise profusely for not bringing me a gift. She went on to tell me that she had been so busy she had left no time to buy a present.

"And what were you busy doing?" I enquired with a teasing smile for I had begun to suspect what had kept her so preoccupied.

"Well, I wasn't going to tell you," she reluctantly replied. "I did a little bit of cooking for your family."

"But that is a truly splendid gift," I scolded her. "That's one of the best gifts you could give - the gift of Help. I was worried about how they would manage and now I don't have to worry anymore! How can I ever thank you?"

She left soon afterwards and I lay reflecting on how wonderful it was to have friends who understood what those in the Healing Rooms really needed. My thoughts were interrupted by yet another visitor, one of the Master's shepherds. After a rich time of fellowship together, talking of the Master and the wonder of His being and the mystery of His ways, he gave his gift to me.

It was small but surprisingly heavy. I opened the box to find a beautiful bottle.

"Oh," I breathed, "you have been to the Master's Perfumery!"

I removed the golden stopper and immediately a sweet fragrance filled the air and brought comfort and peace to my heart. I looked at the perfume bottle to find its name - it was Prayer. As the shepherd prayed for me, the beautiful aroma spread through the whole ward and those around me were blessed and renewed by his gift.

Late that night when the others were asleep, I told the Master about my day, thanked Him for sending my visitors and praised Him that they had so refreshed and encouraged me.

Helps

The gift of Helps is overlooked,
In the general scheme of things,
We loudly praise the one who plays,
And compliment the one who sings.

The gift of healing leaves us stunned,
We gaze in awe at preachers great,
Respect the one who prophesies,
Obey what elders wise dictate.

But when we face our toughest tests,
When sick, in pain, lonely or sad,
It's those who use the gift of helps,
Who ease the worry, make us glad.

So if you cannot sing a song,
Or preach with fire, or play by ear,
Just thank the Lord that you can help,
A load to share, a heart to cheer.

The Operating Room

The Master came to my bedside one morning in the early hours just after dawn.

"We need to talk," He said, and something in His tone made my heart beat faster and my stomach lurch with apprehension.

"Since you have been staying in My Healing Rooms, you have undergone many, varied tests," He began.

"Yes indeed," I agreed ruefully, "I've been poked and prodded, hooked up to the latest technology, and had blood removed from every possible vein."

"Well," the Master continued, choosing His words with care, "the tests confirmed something which has been causing Me concern for quite a while now."

"What is it?" I enquired fearfully, "what is wrong?"

"Your general health is good," the Master spoke reassuringly, "and that is one of the reasons that I'm prepared to go ahead...."

"Go ahead - with what?" By this time I was shivering with fear and fighting a rising wave of nausea.

"A heart transplant."

I couldn't believe the words I had just heard.

"A heart transplant? But there's nothing wrong with my heart!" I protested angrily.

"Listen, child, just listen to what I have to say. I have walked with you for many years now and I know you well. Little one - you have a cold heart, a hard heart, a stony heart."

"I have watched you pull back from the suffering of others, refuse to read stories of tragedy or distress. I have seen you switch off the television when refugees walked across the screen. I have heard you change the topic when the conversation turned to the hardship of others."

His accusations could not be denied and once again I felt the sharp stab of guilt that came each time I was in the situations He had described.

"But Master, I only do those things because I am so afraid of the pain. I'm afraid my heart will break, that if I allow the tears to come, it will be impossible to stem the flow."

"I know," He said, "I know - but that is why I must give you a new heart. I can only use a contrite heart, a soft heart. Just give me your consent."

He held out a form for me to sign and in fear and trembling, I wrote my name in the place He indicated.

He called a porter who wheeled me in my bed out of the ward, down a long corridor and through two overlapping doors that seemed to be made of thick, transparent plastic.

The Master had arrived before us.

"This is My Operating Room," He said, indicating a bare, sterile room, dominated by a high table in the centre. I had often imagined that such a room would smell of antiseptic and disinfectant so I was puzzled by the absence of any smell at all.

The Master responded to my question before I formed the words. "The air in My Operating Room is continually changed and filtered so it never retains an odour. It is cleaner and purer than anywhere else in My House. When My surgeon, the Holy Spirit performs this operation, it will be done in an atmosphere of absolute purity. No infection is allowed to enter the wound while He does His work."

He helped me on to the hard, uncomfortable table, checked my position carefully, then gently touched my forehead.

From that moment, I knew no more for several hours. What took place in that room I never knew. I can only say that the Holy Spirit did His work. I never asked Him to explain what had been accomplished for I sensed that it had been so deep and complex an operation that I could not have hoped to understand it.

I awoke to pain - fierce, searing pain that lasted several days but as the healing took place, I began to realize that my new soft heart was beating well. I now viewed the pain that was so evident all around me, with His tenderness and His compassion. The tears of which I had been so afraid, did flow but far from breaking my heart, the tears served to keep it soft and tender. His mercy enabled me to bear the pain that comes from looking on pain and His grace gave me the strength to reach out and share the pain I could see in others, to know, albeit momentarily, what He meant by the "fellowship of His suffering".

A Soft Heart

Lord, I'm not sure
About soft hearts.
Soft hearts are easily hurt -
Easily bruised,
Easily wounded.
Soft hearts feel most pain.

Why should I ask
For a soft heart?
When the price is so high -
An endless ache,
Stirred emotions.
Soft hearts cry most tears.

I'm afraid, my Lord,
Of a soft heart.
Soft hearts are always moved -
Moved by love,
Moved to action.
Soft hearts get used.

So do I walk the road
Of service, pain and tears,
Or keep my heart of stone
Give in to all my fears?

And do I close my eyes
To other people's pain,
Or do I turn to see
And feel the hurt again?

You didn't walk away
You saw and met man's need,
You loved the most unlovely,
Your heart was soft indeed.

Come, by Your Spirit's fire,
Soften my hardened heart,
Fill it with tenderness divine,
God's love in every part.

Isolation Ward

While my wound was healing, the Master's staff cared for me with great patience and understanding. They were on call at the touch of a button, night or day. Nothing ever seemed to be too much trouble, no request for help or comfort was ever ignored.

The days passed pleasantly enough. I had time to find and learn many of the promises that the Master had assured me would build up my faith. I had time to chat to other patients in the ward and to hear their stories of the Master's great faithfulness.

The nights were a different story. I found it hard to sleep for, despite the best efforts of the night staff, the ward was not a restful place. The quiet of the night hours was too often broken by the loud insistent beeps from drips that needed to be replaced or were not flowing freely or by the clatter of a trolley bringing a new admission. There were whispered conversations as patients were attended to and usually just as I began to fall asleep, the medicine trolley was wheeled in with a hearty "Good morning, folks!"

As I tossed and turned in the bed one night, irritated by the brightness of the emergency exit light that shone like a beacon in my eyes, I became aware of sounds of pain and distress from a side ward close by. When I talked with the Master in the morning I asked him about the person who was suffering so much.

"Come," He said, "lean on my arm and I will help you to walk to his room."

He brought me to a large window and gestured to the one who lay on the bed in the small room beyond. I saw a young man, weak and frail looking. He was attached to various drips and drains and lay softly moaning with pain.

"He seems to be very ill. What happened?" I enquired.

"It all began some time ago. He was wounded, not by the enemy's dart, but by a friend, another brother. The wound was not too deep but instead of coming to my Emergency Room to have it cleaned and bound by love, he attempted to deal with it himself. He wiped it down with an old cloth and tried to ignore the pain."

"But if it was such a small wound," I interrupted, "why is he so ill now?"

The Master gazed at the young man rather wistfully and after a moment or two continued His story.

"He allowed the infection of bitterness and resentment to enter the wound and it spread very rapidly through his whole body. He was being slowly poisoned by it."

I glanced just then at the door and walked over to read the notice pinned to it. Written in heavy black type were the words 'No entry except to authorised personnel.'

"What is the meaning of the notice?" I asked the Master.

"This is an isolation ward," He explained. "Bitterness is very infectious. I have had to isolate him from the rest of My people in case he passes it on to them. It spreads so rapidly that soon there would be an epidemic and many lives would be ruined."

"Will the treatment work?"

"If he allows it to, it will. Each day when he talks to me, a little of the resentment and the bitterness is taken away by the drains. The drips are feeding tolerance and forgiveness into his life. If he allows My forgiveness to flow freely and to touch his heart, then perhaps he will be able also to forgive. His healing depends on it."

I stood at the window and watched the young man and wondered if he had ever fully understood how much the Master had forgiven him and prayed that he would soon realise that only forgiveness heals bitterness.

I watched the little bags of tolerance and forgiveness slowly release their life changing drops into his veins and I marvelled afresh at the long-suffering, loving nature of the Master.

Let Down

They let me down,
Missed appointments,
Did not measure up,
Were such disappointments.

I placed my trust
In their eager hands:
Their fingers opened -
Trust spilt in the sands.

Why hurt me so?
Cease helpfulness?
Why choose this time?
I'm under such stress.

I want to hit out,
I'm angry and sad.
What thought can uplift
And make my heart glad?

Christ felt this pain,
Deserted by all,
Compared to His,
My grief is small

So help me forgive -
He did from the Cross,
Help turn into gain,
What seems to be loss.

Opthalmics

For three mornings in a row, when the Master had come to talk to me, I had wanted to tell Him about my problem but found it difficult to talk about my fears, as though by refusing to express them, they would somehow prove to be unfounded. It was, of course, foolish to imagine that I could conceal how I felt from the Master.

"What's troubling you, child?" He enquired. "Is your wound causing you pain?"

"No," I answered quickly, "my wound is healing well. I can walk a little further each day. It's nothing to do with my wound. I'm afraid...... I think....." my voice wavered and He reached out to take my hand in His.

"Just tell me what is worrying you," He said gently, "voicing your fears is the first step to overcoming them."

I took a deep breath. "I'm afraid that I might be losing my sight. Sometimes it's hard to see Your face clearly," I admitted.

The Master smiled reassuringly. "That is a very common problem," He said. "Let's go to another room. We may be able to help you."

He led me down a long corridor, past many rooms where His servants were lovingly binding up wounds, helping to heal broken hearts and mending ruined lives. As we walked, I asked Him about all the people who served Him in this part of His House.

"I appointed each one to work here," He said. "These are My healers, My comforters, My counsellors. They are very special people, chosen to help others and endowed by My spirit with particular gifts to empower them for this ministry. Many of them have known suffering too, many have spent a long time in My healing rooms. Their own suffering has given them a special understanding of those in pain, a special compassion for My hurting people."

He stopped just then and opened a door which bore the name "Opthalmics." The room into which He led me was small and dark. A high backed leather chair was positioned against one wall and the Master indicated that I should sit in it. He took His seat at a desk nearby.

"Many of My people," He began, "have some sort of problem with their vision. Very few can see My face clearly, and almost everyone has problems seeing My purposes. There are two common causes of these problems - one is short sight and the other is long sight. Let me test you for these first."

He switched on a screen on the opposite wall and asked me to read what was written there. He placed heavy metal frames on my face and fitted lenses of various strengths into them, all the time asking questions to find out if they sharpened my focus. Then He shone an intense bright light into each eye in turn.

"Well," He said finally, "you are neither short sighted nor long sighted. I have many soldiers out in the battle who are so short sighted that they cannot see beyond themselves and the little group of soldiers right besides them. They have no idea how the battle is going and have no interest in finding out the strategies of their commander."

"Other soldiers are so long sighted that they see only the end of the battle and all their energies are absorbed in gaining victory. Sometimes they are so intent on winning the battle and so enthusiastic about the battle they don't realise that they are actually wounding their fellow soldiers. These are common problems that can be cured by wearing the special lens of Awareness to correct their vision."

"Some, of course, are too proud to admit that they have a problem and some are too afraid of what they might see should their vision improve and so they struggle on with impaired sight, stumbling now and then as a result."

"What of my own problem?" I asked.

"Yours requires a more complicated procedure to correct but it is a common enough problem in those who have walked with me for a long time. A cataract is beginning to form and you were right to be afraid of losing your vision. That is what would happen if the cataract is not removed."

I was dismayed when I considered the implications of what the Master had told me.

"What caused it.... how did it happen?"

"It could have been a number of things - tradition, legalism, arrogance, fear of change can all cloud the vision. You will know if you look in your heart. Now child, let's deal with the cataract."

I closed my eyes and felt Him gently touch first one eye then the other. It seemed as though scales fell from them, removing in a moment all that had dimmed my sight.

I looked into His face and felt joy rise in my heart. I saw there such beauty, such grace, such majesty that I could only hold His gaze for a moment. I bowed my head in worship and breathed His Name in adoration.

"When I removed the cataract," He told me, "I placed in your eyes special lenses of Revelation. There will be many moments like the one you have just experienced, breath-taking moments when I will reveal to you glimpses of My glory, moments when you will look in My face and find yourself overwhelmed by the power and majesty you see there."

I could only whisper "Thanks Master," amazed that the Sovereign Lord of the universe should choose to reveal His nature and character to me, filled with excited anticipation as I contemplated the prospect of further glimpses of His glory.

Give me eyes, give me ears

Give me eyes that are open to Your grace,
Give me eyes of faith to look upon Your face,
I long to see what others cannot see,
The richer sights of inner, true reality.
The fulness of Your joy, the wonder of Your peace,
Mercy so amazing, love that will never cease,
The glory of Your power, by Your Spirit giv'n to me,
Such splendid visions, Lord, these I long to see.

Give me ears that are open to Your word,
Give me ears of faith to listen to my Lord.
I long to hear what others cannot hear,
The still, small voice when God the Lord draws near.
Your voice that says, "I love you, you are mine."
That gives me courage in the darkest time.
Your voice that fills with joy or makes me shed a tear,
Your voice and no one else's I would hear.

So touch these eyes and make them see,
The wonders that my God would show to me.
And touch these ears and make them hear
The words my Lord would say when He is near.

... welcome to the Nursery ...

Maternity Ward

My stay in the Healing Rooms had almost come to an end. My wound had healed, my new heart was beating to His rhythm and my enhanced vision gave constant delight to my soul. I was ready to return to the battle.

The Master arrived just as I was packing up to go.

"Before you leave My Healing Rooms," He said, "I want to show you a special place in this wing of My House, a place of great happiness and joy. Come, let's go together."

We walked past some of the wards that I had already visited and eventually arrived at a corridor that was decorated in a manner quite unlike the rest. The usual white gloss paint had been replaced by murals of balloons and clowns with painted cheeks and red noses, cute bears and mischievous puppies.

I was admiring the pictures and thinking to myself how cheerful it all looked, and how glad I was to visit this happy ward, when I became aware once again of sounds of pain and distress coming from either side of the corridor.

I looked at the Master almost accusingly, "I thought You said this was a place of great happiness and joy! Why can I hear people suffering? This is just another place of pain!"

I was about to enter one of the rooms when the Master stopped me.

"No," He said, "we'll come back to these rooms later. Go on into the room straight ahead."

Feeling rather disappointed at the way things were turning out, I walked slowly to the door and looked inside.

The room was bright and cheerful, painted in a pale pastel shade and I could sense a warm, joyous atmosphere. My eyes were drawn to one young woman, who was lying back on her pillows, looking quite exhausted yet strangely contented.

I started to ask the Master for an explanation but He motioned me to be quiet.

"Just watch," He said with a smile.

At that moment a nurse went to the young woman's bedside and very gently placed a tiny bundle into her arms.

"It's a little baby," I whispered, "she's just had a baby."

The woman reached out her arms and so tenderly and so lovingly took her child from the nurse and cuddled him closely. I watched her face as she looked down and ran her finger lightly down his soft cheek and such was the look of love that lit up her eyes that my heart ached with longing to know the joy she was experiencing.

I felt tears fill my eyes and turned to share my longing with the Master and in His eyes I saw that same intensity of love.

"A new life," He said softly, "a new creation, a new child for My kingdom. I wanted you to see the joy first - now I can show you the other rooms. You have to see them in the light of the joy."

I didn't really want to leave the doorway but obediently followed Him back down the corridor to a door marked "Labour Ward".

As He led me inside He explained, "Bringing new life into My Kingdom is not an easy task. It involves hard work, sometimes a long, difficult labour, sometimes tears and suffering."

But even as I watched those who were labouring to bring new life into the Kingdom and heard their groaning and sighing, I kept remembering the joy and the love and understood why the Master had insisted that I see the joy first.

He then brought me across to the other room from which I had heard sounds of great distress and, throwing open the door with a smile, He said,

"Welcome to the Nursery. The cries of distress you heard previously were actually cries of hunger! The babies have been well fed and now they're sleeping peacefully."

"They're so beautiful. It's all such a wonderful miracle. Oh, how I wish........."

The Master reached out to touch my arm,

"I understand your longing and one day you will know the joy of bringing new life into My Kingdom," He assured me.

"When that happens," He continued, "remember this! Remember how hungry these newborn babies are. Remember to give them plenty of nourishing milk. Don't try to give them solid food until they're ready. It's best to feed them a little, often. Above all, remember to love them - love them as I love you."

I could only nod, too choked with emotion to speak, as I remembered with great affection, those who had nourished me in the days that followed my arrival at the Gate of His House.

"Can I take one last look before I go?" I asked.

He nodded His consent and I made my way to the doorway of the Maternity Ward to gaze once more at the mother and her baby. She held him as though she would never let him go and as I watched, she began to rock him gently in her arms then softly sang to him a beautiful lullaby.

The Master's voice was quiet, but very clear, "This is what My Kingdom is all about. This is what makes the battle worthwhile. This is the reason for the cross at the Gate. This is the fulfilment of all My purposes - to bring new life into My Kingdom, to see My people grow into My likeness, to bring many sons to glory. Carry this picture with you when you leave My Healing Rooms."

As I slowly turned to make my way out of the ward I could hear His voice echoing down the corridor and His words rang out like a clarion call,

"In the midst of the battle -
                    remember the joy!"

For These Special Moments

For these special moments when Your love reaches me,
For these times when Your Presence is a known reality,
For these special moments when I feel Your tender care,
For these still, glorious moments when I know that You are there.
When Your Presence surrounds me, fills my heart with joy and praise,
And I think how You have blessed me in so many different ways,
I will just bow in worship to You, my Lord and King,
And for these special moments, Your Praises I'll sing.

In this special moment, my worship I will bring,
In this special moment, I will lift my heart and sing.
As Your love reaches to me and takes away my fear,
As I catch a glimpse of Glory and I know that You are near.
As Your Presence surrounds me and I sense Your gentleness,
As the warmth of Your Presence brings such peace and happiness.
I will whisper, "I love You", a song of praise I'll sing,
And in this special moment, my worship I'll bring.